Healthy Aging, Healthy Treatment

Healthy Aging, Healthy Treatment

The Impact of Telling Stories

Thomas H. Peake

Westport, Connecticut
London

Library of Congress Cataloging-in-Publication Data

Peake, Tom H.
    Healthy aging, healthy treatment : the impact of telling stories /
Thomas H. Peake.
       p.   cm.
    Includes bibliographical references and index.
    ISBN 0–275–95922–8 (alk. paper)
      1. Aged—Medical care. 2. Aging—Psychological aspects.
3. Aging—Religious aspects. 4. Holistic medicine. I. Title.
RA564.8.P4   1998
362.1′9897—dc21   97–33704

British Library Cataloguing in Publication Data is available.

Library of Congress Catalog Card Number: 97–33704
ISBN: 0–275–95922–8

First published in 1998

Praeger Publishers, 88 Post Road West, Westport, CT 06881
An imprint of Greenwood Publishing Group, Inc.

Printed in the United States of America

The paper used in this book complies with the
Permanent Paper Standard issued by the National
Information Standards Organization (Z39.48–1984).

10 9 8 7 6 5 4 3 2 1

For my family whose patience, humor and understanding have shaped my perspective across the years.

Contents

Contents viii

Acknowledgments

The following people helped greatly in the inspiration and preparation of this book: Lori Sorum, Kelly Blair, Susan Rosenzweig, Gordon Patterson, Frank Webbe, Jim Oelschlager, William Hedrick, Bill Lewis, Carmen Fernandez, Jessica Casey, Bridget Martin, Karl Sachs, Gene Shepherd, Jay Chrostowski, Richard Houskamp, Charles Prokop, Carol Philpot, Fabi Lufschanowski, Tracey Meyers, Vicki Ingram, Tina Decker, Michelle Nuemann Carroll, Gerald Showalter, Carol Waters, Jennifer Hughes, Norene Rooney, Barbara Warner, Stuart Lieberman, Dan MacKay and Daisy Peake.

All names and identifying details of the clinical examples in this book have been changed to protect the identity of those involved.

Introduction

Twice Told Tales: Lives Recalled and Lives Renewed

In our language, the term *storytelling* may stir both fond and foul memories. Both connotations will be considered in this book.

Childhood memories of a parent telling or reading bedtime stories conjures up images of closeness and caring. The associations flow from this special human interaction marked by magical possibilities of adventure, intrigue, fear, renewal and hope. At any age the process of genuinely listening and telling about surprises, fears and hopes creates an intimacy rarely matched in human interaction, and constitutes a special kind of love and honoring. The narrative adventure may include sharing a legacy, rethinking a past dilemma or giving advice for the future. Good stories jangle and tickle all the senses while forging a lasting relationship between hearer and teller. Often having hearers and tellers from different generations further magnifies this special exchange. Life's seasons and storylines appear different from the vantage of different ages and stages. Wise stories from older adults can light the path of life's twists and turns. Listening thoughtfully helps both listener and teller.

This book is an invitation to the engaging and reforming power of telling stories, reminiscence and narrative. Human stories form the core of identity and meaning. The personal meaning shapes the identity of individuals, families and cultures. Stories are versions of what has been, what has gone well or wrong and what can be. By hearing and telling these stories identities are formed, challenged by life and (re)consolidated. A psychologist, G. S. Howard (1991), suggests that a person's identity may be thought of as story construction. Psychological or physical illness might be thought of as a story gone awry. And psychotherapy, as well as other forms of healing, may be considered story repair. Through this process, a person's life history and fate can be reconsidered, retold, reframed and renewed.

Storytelling or story tending creates a rich tapestry that may be honoring, intimate, intriguing, drudgery, shaming, dramatic, hopeful or renewing. Birren and Deutchman (1991) in their book about conducting autobiographical groups for older adults, describe the process as "exploring the fabric of life." This process of hearing and telling is important for individuals, families, cultures and healers. The best stories have meaning at all stages of life and across both generations and cultures. Certain fairy tales, bible stories, myths or legends convey timeless values and dilemmas in a way that is easy to grasp. Bettelheim (1976) calls this transforming magic "the uses of enchantment."

On the other hand, the term *storytelling* can be negative. It may mean telling lies, distortions or falsehoods. We often talk about "a telling story" as a warning that something is ominous, revealing, suspicious, dangerous or ironic. Part of this book is about health care for older adults. Unfortunately, in the United States and the United Kingdom health care is often a telling story; it is not what it ought to be. The story of health care delivery is sometimes a conundrum of ageist, fractionated, cost-containing and guild-guarding controversy. The treatment of *third ager's* (seniors) suffers if acute medical care is funded disproportionately more than prevention and recovery. The telling story of health care can be retold with an informed and reformed reminder. People are most happy and robust when health professionals not only ply their specialty, but also honor and address their needs in psychological and spiritual (as well as physical) dimensions. Through a process of listening to seniors, to families, to other professionals and to our own research and clinical experience, we can offer hopeful new stories of healthy treatment and healthy aging.

HEALING STORIES

The author, a psychologist, was once working with an elderly couple in which the wife had Alzheimer's Disease. In one meeting the husband, asked me this disturbing question, "What will we do when the

experts are gone?" Fearful that I would have to suggest some meaningful answer, I was relieved and informed by the man's answer to his own
question. He proceeded to tell his wife, his grown children and me stories of the last years of the couple's own parents. It was a sad, wonderful and hopeful account of a family's ways of sharing love and meaning
beyond death and human limits. It also put into perspective value and
the limitation of science and medicine.

Another question the family might have asked, could be,
"What will happen to us when the experts are here?" This book considers an ethic of health and health care for older adults, as inspired by Viktor Frankl (1973) and Jerome Frank's (1991) suggestions that healing
should include physical, psychological and spiritual dimensions. The
search is also inspired by the wisdom of individuals, families and cultures *telling stories* about their lives, their history, heritage, tragedies
and aspirations. Several writers champion the important difference and
healing advantage of an informed yet caring health care. These writers
include clinicians, physicians, poets, clergy and anthropologists
(including Erikson, 1982; Howard, 1991; Kaufman, 1986; Maclay,
1977; Viney, 1993; Wettle, 1989). The healing approach they advance
encourages people to tell their life story (a narrative that also shapes
life's meaning) in contrast to a health care approach which merely
"takes a clinical history" and treats but one dimension of health.

Three cultures (medical, psychological and spiritual) are involved in the challenge of health and healing. It is rare to find an institution or system where the three cultures exert a balanced influence.
There may even be suspicion or derision between the professionals in
each guild or culture. The ideology and implementation of America's
variegated health care system(s) often overemphasize biomedical aspects
of illness and treatment (Estes and Binney, 1989). Psychology may
deny, underestimate or underuse the spiritual/religious dimension of
health. Family, spiritual and religious communities may distrust the
medical or psychological professions. Health care is, after all, political
and economic big business. Health care is not a healthy system itself
(Callahan, 1995; Kiesler, 1992; Konner, 1993; Orient, 1994; Seuss,
1986).

Cultural environments and health care systems that devalue or
overvalue one of the three dimensions (body, mind or spirit) can dilute
healing or damage health (Wettle, 1989). Our childhood friend, Dr.
Seuss (1986), in his classic humor and insight captures the tragicomedy

of the elder as health care victim. While Kiesler (1992) and Estes and Binney (1989) describe what may happen if the other dimensions of health and healing merely mimic a biomedical approach.

Examples drawn from clinical experience, narrative, art, humor and research will be used to locate and suggest models of health and treatment that integrate mind, body and spirit. Impediments to integrating these cultures and dimensions in existing health care will be reviewed. We did research using a Delphi (expert informant) procedure to glean the needs, goals and problems of existing health care systems. This Delphi research process has also been described as a "policy capturing," or a heuristic directive. We did parallel studies sampling health care experts from the United States and the United Kingdom. The participants provided their thoughts about needs, problems and possible redirections to create optimal health and health care for older adults. The findings of similarities and differences, advantages and disadvantages of these two systems, help us recommend changes. We will consider ways to balance and integrate all the dimensions of health. A healthier story for the health care of older adults should emerge.

Senior adults and their families have a lifetime (and often generations) of experience, loss and growth (Kaufman, 1986; Kerr and Bowen, 1988; Viorst, 1986). This wisdom can be mobilized for the challenges of later life (Erikson, 1982) if healers and leaders can (a) learn to mobilize all three dimensions of growth and healing, (b) teach others this science, faith and craft of health, and (c) shape informed and caring families, spirited communities and humane health systems. Older adults have much wisdom to inform and heal health professionals as well as themselves. Implications for the training of health professionals may be suggested from these mature adults.

We hope this book challenges and informs concerned medical, psychological and spiritual professionals. Caregivers may find the book thoughtful, troubling and entertaining. The idea of telling stories addresses the importance of narrative means to therapeutic ends. Telling stories also describes the ways that ill-conceived health care systems can fractionalize and compromise elder health and health care. Our real goal is to locate and promote qualities, people and places where three-dimensional health and health care occur. The importance of helping older adults achieve a balance of continuity and change in their lives is an inspiring way to conceive of health, health care and psychotherapy.

PREVIEW

The chapters that follow explore several variations on the theme of stories. The first chapter suggests "Considerations for Health Professionals," and previews the principles that are developed throughout the book. The next chapter, "A Tale of Three Cultures: Medicine, Psychology, and Religion," argues that medicine, psychology and religion represent three distinct cultures. In principle, these cultures of body, mind and spirit should be interactive dimensions that promote health and healthy treatment. In reality, the three dimensions may be more like three competing guilds. Each culture has its own cultural tales. Each has its own hierarchy and a need to preserve its own identity. Hopefully a better understanding of these cultures of health and healing can create a spirit of cooperation between the guilds and produce a balanced story of body, mind and spirit.

Chapter three, "Healthy Models: Principles and Places," explores aspirations for and places where treatment is healthy. Actual programs are described which embody a balance of psychological, physical and spiritual health and healing. In order to expand our awareness of programs where healthy treatment and growth occur, we invite the reader to consider these principles and tell us about other places where health and healing occur in balance.

The fourth chapter explores "Healthy Stories and Aging Well." These stories reveal principles that promote health by striking a balance between continuity and change across the lifespan. The stories are about individuals, about relationships (friendship, love and intimacy), families and cross-generational principles of health and meaning. A central theme is that a successful balance of stabilizing and changing promotes creativity in individuals, in relationships and in works of art. The ability to balance form and passion (May 1975) produces the most creative works, relations and lives. Good literature, music and art chronicle tragedies and triumphs. Similarly, people can create and revise fascinating life stories.

The fifth chapter, "Story Tending: Leit Motifs, Hunches, Hopes and Fears," examines the narrative wisdom of some people we have known. We explore the meaning of lives as they emerge from people's core hopes and fears. Personal narratives attempt to make sense of the twists and turns of life. In this chapter the meaning of illness and healing is considered in a more personal way. Also the core beliefs and core motifs that propel or hamper people's journeys through life are sampled. This concept of core beliefs and core motives is central to good counseling and psychotherapy. A combination of quotations is used to immerse the reader in the personal meanings we attribute to and tell about ourselves and our relations. Personal aphorisms plus haunting beliefs and meanings are sketched. These convictions show how core beliefs and dymanics guide our lives. Sometimes we discover and sometimes we ignore these life motives we create. They guide us nonetheless. Effective psychotherapy can provide a clearer picture of motives, tragedies, triumphs and options for plot revisions.

Chapter six, "Healing and Illness Stories," considers the reality of illness, hope and healing in a personal way. We provide examples of both healthy and unhealthy interactions with health care systems. Then, Chapter seven explores "Health Care Systems in the United States and the United Kingdom: A Telling Story." This chapter reviews and summarizes the results of our Delphi research which compares and contrasts the structure, application and effectiveness of these two health systems. The Delphi research is based on a sampling of experienced health professionals working with older adults in these two countries.

The last chapter reviews and recommends "Implications for Health Professionals." The storylines developed in the prior chapters are used to suggest new themes and plots for a healthy story of health care. We suggest that health professionals who are "aware and concerned" (Strupp, 1996) are in the best position to write a balanced story for health and health care. The balance of body, mind and spirit must occur at several different levels. The individual caregiver must not only appreciate, but also help create an integration of *third agers'* needs in all three spheres. Health professionals and health administrators must create environments where the cultures or guilds of treatment not only pursue the best of their specialty, but also honor the value of the three cultures of medicine, psychology and religion. The demons that foil optimal health include ageism, limited resources, guild-preserving motives and an underappreciation of the three dimensions of healthy aging. Caring involves listening to and understanding the people we treat. There is a "love that listens" to the life events, losses, aspirations, hopes and fears, and life stories of people and families. There is a wisdom in honoring and learning from the people we treat. Health care that honors the three human dimensions provides the best care for those we serve.

Wise tales of body, mind and spirit can create a healing ethic for health care systems and health professionals.

WORKS CITED

Atchley, R. C. (1989). A continuity theory of normal aging. *The Gerontologist, 29,* 183–190.

Bettelheim, B. (1976). *The uses of enchantment.* New York: Vintage.

Blazer, D. (1991). Spirituality and aging well. *Generations, 15,* 61–65.

Booth, W. C. (1992). Criticism and the pursuit of character. *Journal of Medical Humanities, 13,* 67–78.

Boyle, N. (1992). Managed care as seen by a patient. *Psychiatric News,* September 18, 1992.

Callahan, D. (1995). *Setting limits: Medical goals in an aging society.* Washington, D.C.: Georgetown University Press.

Carter, E. and McGoldrick, M. (eds.) (1989). *The changing family life cycle.* New York: Gardner Press.

Chinen, A. B. (1989). *In the ever after: Fairy tales for the second half of life.* Wilmette, Ill.: Chiron Publishers.

Coles, R. (1989). *The call of stories: Teaching and the moral imagination.* Boston: Houghton Mifflin.

Cousins, N. (1990). *Head first.* New York: Penguin.

Davis, D. (1993). *Telling your own stories.* Little Rock, Ark.: August House.

Dossey, L. (1993). *Healing words: The power of prayer and the practice of medicine.* New York: HarperCollins.

Eisdorfer, C., Kessler, D. and Spector, A. N. (1989). *Caring for the elderly: Reshaping health policy.* Baltimore: Johns Hopkins University Press.

Epston, D. and White, M. (1989). *Literate means to therapeutic ends.* Adelaide, Australia: Dulwich Center Publishers.

Erikson, E. (1982). *The life cycle completed.* New York: W. W. Norton.

Estes, C. L. and Binney, E. A. (1989). The biomedicalization of aging: Dangers and dilemmas. *The Gerontologist, 29,* 587–596.

Framo, I. L. (1992). *Family of origin therapy: An intergenerational approach.* New York: Brunner/Mazel.

Frank, J. D. and Frank, J. B. (1991). *Persuasion and healing: A comparative study of psychotherapy.* Baltimore: Johns Hopkins University Press.

Frankl, V. (1973). *The doctor and the soul.* New York: Vintage.

Friedan, B. (1993). *The fountain of age.* New York: Simon and Schuster.

Gatz, M. and Smyer, M. A. (1992). The mental health system and older adults. *American Psychologist, 47,* 741–751.

Gilligan, C. (1982). *In a different voice: Psychological theory and women's development.* Cambridge, Mass.: Harvard University Press.

Howard, G. S. (1991). Culture tales: A narrative approach to thinking, cross-cultural psychology, and psychotherapy. *American Psychologist, 46,* 187–197.

Josselson, R. and Lieblich, A. (1993). *The narrative study of lives.* Newbury Park, Calif.: Sage.

Jung, C. G. (1963). *Modern man in search of a soul.* New York: Harcourt, Brace and World.

Kaufman, S. (1986). *The ageless self: Sources of meaning in late life.* New York: Meridian.

Kerr, M. E. and Bowen, M. (1988). *Family evaluation: An approach based on Bowen theory.* New York: W. W. Norton.

Kiesler, C. A. (1992). U.S. Mental health policy: Doomed to fail. *American Psychologist, 47,* 1077–1082.

Kleinman, A. (1988). *The illness narratives.* New York: Basic Books.

Konner, M. (1993). *Medicine at the crossroads.* New York: Pantheon.

Konner, M. (1987). *Becoming a doctor: A journey of initiation in medial school.* New York: Viking.

Maclay, E. (1977). *Green winter: Celebrations of old age.* New York: McGraw-Hill.

May, R. (1991). *The cry for myth.* New York: W. W. Norton.

May, R. (1975). *The courage to create.* New York: W. W. Norton.

Millard, P. H. (1991). A case for the development of *gerocomy* in all district general hospitals. *Journal of the Royal Society of Medicine, 84,* 731–733.

Moore, T. (1992). *Care of the soul.* New York: HarperCollins.

Naughten, G. and Laidler, T. (1991). *When I grow too old to dream: Coping with Alzheimer's disease.* North Blackburn, Australia: Collins Dove (HarperCollins).

Nichols, M. P. (1995). *The lost art of listening.* New York: Guilford Press.

Omer, H. (1993). Short-term psychotherapy and the rise of the life-sketch. *Psychotherapy, 30,* 668–673.

Orient, J. (1994). *Your doctor is not in.* New York: Crown.

Peake, T. H., Borduin, C. M. and Archer, R. P. (1988). *Brief psychotherapies: Changing frames of mind.* Beverly Hills, Calif.: Sage.

Peake, T. H. and Philpot, C. (1991). Psychotherapy with older adults: Hopes and fears. *The Clinical Supervisor, 9,* 185–202.

Seuss, Dr. (1986). *You're only old once!* New York: Random House.

Stoddard, S. (1992). *The hospice movement: A better way of caring for the dying.* New York: Vintage.

Stone, R. (1994). *Stories: The family legacy.* Maitland, Fla.: Story Work Institute Press.

Strupp, H. H. (1996). The tripartite model and the *Consumer Reports* study. *American Psychologist, 51,* 1017–1024.

Viney, L. L. (1993). *Life stories: Personal construct therapy with the elderly.* New York: John Wiley.

Viorst, J. (1986). *Necessary losses.* New York: Ballantine.

Wettle, T. (1989). Age as a risk factor for inadequate treatment. *Journal of the American Medical Association, 258,* 516.

Wulf, D. M. (1991). *Psychology of religion: Classic and contemporary views.* New York: John Wiley.

1

Considerations for Health Professionals

This chapter previews themes and principles of good treatment developed throughout the book. If treatment ignores ethics, the highest standard practice, or if the interactions of body, mind and spirit are ignored, then health care is not healthy. The practice of medicine is an amazing, powerful and positive force, but it can also be harmful. Similarly, the practice of psychotherapy is inspired and at times life-saving; psychotherapy can be harmful as well as healing. The literature on qualities that lead to harmful or iatrogenic medical practice (Mays and Franks, 1985; Sachs, 1993; Strupp, Hadley and Gomes-Schwartz, 1985) suggests that the best guarantee for healthy treatment is a professional who is both *aware* and *concerned*—aware of the dimensions that promote healing, and concerned that values and morality in health care are as important as the "scientific" aspects of treatment. We suggest four principles to ensure that health professionals are *aware* of the essential dimensions of healing and *concerned* that a moral balance of the dimensions is applied.

Principles for health professionals, especially psychotherapists, who work with older adults are recommended. We use psychotherapy as the arena of treatment; however, we also draw on principles that apply to the domains of medicine and spirituality.

The two distinct and sometimes competing themes in this book are healthy aging and healthy treatment. One theme is that the healthiest people in life's third age have been able to preserve an enduring sense of identity in their life story. This is rarely an easy task since it requires balancing change and continuity across the stages of life. There are countless challenges to this personal or family plot development. Fortunately, resilience and emotional health are often the result of these life challenges. The second theme aspires to heal health care to make the story of health care delivery a wiser tale. This story blends the medical, psychological and spiritual dimensions of healing characterized by wisdom, skill and concern, while devoid of ageism. The business of medicine and health struggles with the tension between seemingly unlimited scientific and technological advances balanced against the harsh reality of limited fiscal resources. The crucial yet unanswered questions are: Who sets the limits, and how are those resources allocated?

A third theme, the minimal interference principle, promises to help balance tensions between the other two themes. This strategy offers an elegant unifying simplicity. Minimal interference means aggressive and decisive treatment, but no more treatment than necessary. This least obtrusive strategy honors peoples' sense of worth, their life struggles and triumphs, and builds on the personal and family strengths developed across the lifespan. Applications of the principle are suggested throughout the book.

Healthy aging can be a theme woven through one's life and even across generations. Third agers can preserve meaning and purpose through a life story reconsidered and revised as needed. Life story repair may come in response to joy, challenge, loss and growth. The story of health care also periodically needs a rewrite. The antidote for noxious elder health care includes:

•professional caregivers who are aware and concerned
•integrity, knowledge and commitment
•ethical and informed decisions about resource allocation

Whose role is it to revise stories gone awry? For an individual, one's family or friends may heal by the love that listens. Often however, a psychotherapist has special skills that are essential not only to hear but also to create or reclaim a resilient sense of self and hope. Whose job is it to reform an ill health care system? Many concerned advocates may be required. These advocates might include patients, families, senior watchdog groups, legislators and caregivers from medical, psychological and spiritual cultures. All may be needed to hear and reform health care. A concerned, informed and unified vigilance will foster story tending, story repair and the healthiest health care.

PRINCIPLES FOR PSYCHOTHERAPISTS AND HEALTH PROFESSIONALS

The best care for seniors demands an appreciation of informed principles. First, it is important to help people create an enduring identity and a sense of self. Second, there is discontinuity in life from losses, stresses and changes. The healer must appreciate the evolution of themes, dreams and seasons in the lifespan. Also, the interaction of physical, psychological and spiritual dimensions must be understood in balance. The complex interactions of body and mind are equally capable of producing sickness or health. An individual's learned optimism is a prime mover in psychological health. Spiritual clarity is important, coupled with the integrity of the body and its systems in order to promote health and recovery.

Erik Erikson's (1982) model suggests that life's last stage involves an inventory of sorts. This life review (whether conscious or implicit) ponders whether one comes closer to a sense of integrity or to despair about how one's life was spent. The pursuit of integrity (along with humor, knowledge and commitment) gives a us a sextant with which to set our course.

Treating older adults and their families is challenging, humbling and rewarding. It seems that techniques for therapy or counseling are important, but equally crucial are principles that engender hope. Together, technique and hope create a vital way of relating. Qualities that are unique to effective psychotherapy with older patients include the following (Peake & Philpot, 1991).

1.   A grasp of human development is essential. Both individual and family developmental cycles light the path. This lifespan landscape includes somatic, spiritual and psychosocial aspects of aging.

2.   The therapist must have an appreciation for the impact of losses. The ways we engage, ignore or absorb loss and change affect our ability to grow and heal. Mobilizing

the patient's best life options and proven life strategies is the heart of the healing task.

3.   Careful attention must be paid to the difference between normal and pathological aging, as well as to the interaction of physical and psychological aspects of aging. The symptom cannot be separated from the person. Individuals, families and cultures interact in complex ways that sometimes hurt and sometimes help a healthy aging. Sir William Osler often said that it is more important to know what kind of person has the disease than to know what disease has that person.

4.   The therapist must honor, clarify and preserve an individual's complex identity. We must help people strike a balance between their need for continuity and their need for change. Purpose and meaning in life bolster a sense of worth and hope. Psychology and spirituality are essential for effective medical care.

One other potent dimension of treatment is the minimal interference principle. Do only what is necessary, but do it well. This principle, plainly put, means that the therapist should use a person's earlier successes, past strengths and acquired wisdom to solve current problems and dilemmas. The therapist must quickly come to understand the individual's personal history, successes and failures, and adapt old solutions to new problems. There are periods when people need change in their lives, and there are periods when people need stabilization. Sometimes a loss, a failure or an illness challenges the very foundation of who a person believes himself to be. It is easier to modify an earlier way of identifying or understanding than to create a completely new structure. The minimal interference principle means this process should be as short as possible, while preserving as much of a person's core identity as possible. On the other hand, this means that individuals who have had little success in solving life's earlier challenges will require more time and help to create a structure, a solution or an identity anew.

Therapeutic Stories

Many health professionals (e.g. Borysenko, 1988; Dossey, 1993; Gutmann, 1987; Murphy, 1996; Stoddard, 1992; Vash, 1994) are creating new and rediscovering old ways to reclaim strengths and resources. The approaches draw on all three cultures—medical, spiritual and psychological. The process goes by different names like cure, healing, learned optimism or respiriting. These approaches are an attempt to widen the narrowed vision that accompanies medical practice based on scientific knowledge alone.

We can clarify and preserve a person's unique personal identity across the lifespan. A psychotherapist does this directly with older adults (sometimes also involving their families or friends) by helping them tell and modify their life stories to a state of meaning, satisfaction or acceptance. A physician does this by plying the best practice of medicine with an honoring appreciation for the psyche and spirit of seniors. The idea is to develop an efficient yet ethical continuity of care and a health community that sponsors a person's sense of dignity, self-worth and meaning across generations.

Story Tending

of our patients
of our profession
and our science, art and craft
knowing our strengths and limitations.

Health professionals, especially psychotherapists, cannot long escape the tension between the pressures to reduce health costs and the need to preserve informed yet humane treatment. Such informed health care could be a healing blend of the best contributions which body, mind and spirit have to offer. All three cultures—medicine, psychology and religion—are vitally needed in a balanced way for life's third age, the senior years. Unfortunately, these three cultures may sometimes do more to further their own guild than to honor the contributions of all three dimensions. If health care focuses exclusively on acute medical treatment to cut costs, to the exclusion of prevention and recovery, then the psychological and spiritual dimensions of healing are left out of the equation. Without clear mind and renewed spirit, no amount of money or technology will produce an ethical way to treat people and preserve their personal stories and their personal legacies. Art, science, religion and psychology share a goal: to say or do a thing more clearly and honestly than it's been said or done before. The result advances health, knowledge, freedom and joy.

Health professionals must expand their roles to become students of and advocates for creative solutions. The conundrum to be solved is how to balance ethical, caring, and scientifically informed treatment with limited resources. Voices of wisdom come from different cultures of care and knowledge. Lifelong health and continuity of care happens when health professionals from all three dimensions; body, mind and spirit, value and integrate the best of their own domain.

2

A Tale of Three Cultures:
Medicine, Psychology and Religion

T. H. Peake and K. L. Blair

Western humanity has turned from the priest to the doctor. Nowadays too many patients come to the medical man with problems which should really be put to a priest.

Man lives in three dimensions: the somatic, the mental, and the spiritual. The spiritual dimension cannot be ignored, for it's what makes us human. To be concerned about the meaning of life is not necessarily a sign of disease of the psyche. The proper diagnosis can be made only by someone who can see the spiritual side of man.

I remember my dilemma in a concentration camp when faced with a man and a woman who were close to suicide; both had told me that they expected nothing more from life. I asked both my fellow prisoners whether the question was really what we expected from life. Was it not, rather, what life was expecting from us? I suggested that life was awaiting something from them.

—Viktor Frankl, *The Doctor & the Soul* (1973, preface)

AN ETHIC FOR HEALTH AND HEALTH CARE FOR OLDER ADULTS, IN THREE PARTS

This book is guided by the belief that the health and vitality of older adults is three dimensional. These dimensions are those of body, mind and spirit. Throughout the book we will try to understand the valuable contributions of each of those three dimensions and how the three might best interact to promote healthy living. With that pursuit, we are trying to develop an ethic for health as well as for health care with older adults. Each of the three dimensions of health has its own corner on health and healing.

Medicine continues to make immense contributions to our health. It also involves crucial constraints and difficulties. Another important realization is that medicine has its own culture which influences how medicine is practiced. Similarly psychology makes valuable contributions to health but also has limitations and shortcomings. Psychology has its own peculiar culture that influences the way we learn about and apply our knowledge of the mind and emotions. Religion as a third culture also promotes health. The spiritual dimension of health for older adults is often nestled in an organized religion. Sometimes spirituality is an antireligion; sometimes it is a more personal, ethnic or family matter. Whatever its form, spirituality will have its own culture too. Unfortunately, we find that the three cultures of body, mind and spirit often preserve their own agenda or viewpoint rather than promote a health based on interaction of mind, body and spirit. In developing an ethic for health and health care, we will search for ways to integrate, interweave and promote interaction of the three dimensions. They need each other, and more importantly, we need them.

In the spirit of integrating different cultures and different ways of learning, the book will use an integrative style, including narrative, research and clinical examples, as well as culture tales, quotations and individual life stories. Telling a multidimensional story of health calls for different voices, different vantages and different formats.

It is difficult to get a man to understand something when his salary depends on not understanding it.
—Upton Sinclair

The great majority of us are required to live a life of constant, systematic duplicity. Your health is bound to be af-

fected if, day after day you say the opposite of what you
feel; if you grovel before what you dislike and rejoice at
what brings you nothing but misfortune. Our nervous system isn't just fiction. It's a part of our physical body, and
our soul exists and is inside us, like the teeth in our mouth.
It can't be forever violated without impunity.
        —Boris Pasternak, *Dr. Zhivago*

Simply put, health care should promote health in more than
one dimension; that is the ethic we suggest throughout this book. Unfortunately, health care without an understanding of these multiple dimensions can be unhealthy. We know a great deal about the qualities
of and the settings in which the mind, body and spirit work. If we apply this wisdom, we can ensure a rational and integrated ethic for health
care.

A good place to start is by defining emotional health. Sig-
mund Freud, as modified by other mental health experts, suggested the
following definition for emotional health.

To love fully and passionately,
To work creatively at something that brings
a fullness of purpose and joy, and
To be able to play as children do.

Gerald Caplan, a psychiatrist who pioneered "preventive psychiatry," added a fourth dimension to this definition. He argued that the
first three parts—to love well, work well and play well—need a fourth,
that is, to expect well. A sense of purpose and competence, a sense of
relatedness, and an ability to be spontaneous and even playful are important aspirations. The fourth suggestion, to expect well, is a way of
underlining the importance of an adaptive strength, a resilience and a
realistic expectation that one can shape one's life and future. Seligman
(1991) has described this quality as learned optimism.

Emotional health promotes spiritual and physical health. In
fact, if one takes the mind–body–spirit interaction seriously, it follows
that health gained in any arena will likely contribute to increasing
health in the other arenas. Conversely, deterioration of health in any
one dimension can lead to additional deterioration in the other dimensions. The three dimensions can and do interact, for better or for worse.
Although interrelated for the individual, the three dimensions of health

have their own proponents and practitioners. Similarly, each has its own culture. Unfortunately for the health of the individual and the health care system, one culture may ignore the others. Each of the cultures has its own guild and hierarchy. In addition, the leaders and practitioners within each culture often have a financial or political stake in the primacy of their dimension of health and healing. The different cultures may only rarely speak to each other in a way that makes their interaction possible and their benefit accessible to the people who need their truth, method or meaning. In addition, different societies may value one dimension more highly than others.

In the Western world, we tend to overvalue the biomedical dimension of health care (Estes and Binney, 1989). Certainly, if the percentage of dollars spent on medical health care is considered, the ledger shows more investment in the medical than in either the spiritual or psychological dimension. In most medical settings there is only token appreciation for the value of psychology and religion. In enlightened medical settings, psychological consultation is highly valued and used often. Many treatment programs integrate the psychological with the medical dimensions of diagnosis and treatment. Hospitals generally have chapels, and clergy are involved in the process of calling on the sick. However, places where medical, spiritual and psychological caregivers actually work together in a balanced fashion are all too rare.

The three dimensions of health care can be balanced in creative ways and varied settings. Families, communities and cultural and religious groups can all ensure that spiritual and psychological dimensions are balanced in the lives of older adults and their families. Another way to address this need is to describe the principles that should guide a balanced approach to health and health care. Better yet, finding places, programs and creative strategies with a good balance of body, mind and spirit will be a valuable odyssey indeed. We will consider these places in Chapter three.

Our focus now turns to the cultures of health (medicine, psychology and spirituality) and the inherent advantages and peculiarities of each. One goal is to highlight the strengths of each approach to health care for all older adults. Another goal is to propose an ethic of treatment that balances the best of the physical, psychological and spiritual.

Cultures of Medicine: Aspirations and Realities

Keep far from me the delusion that I can accomplish all
things.
>   —The Physician's prayer; Maimonides,
>   Jewish physician (12th century)

The scope of medicine should encompass prevention, treatment and recovery; however, in the United States, the acute treatment phase gets most of the health care dollar. Procedures to identify the causes and treatment of illness have come a long way. Americans especially have a hope and belief that biological science will conquer all illness given enough financial support (Estes and Binney, 1989). This hope may leave prevention and recovery out of the health equation. In addition, recurrent financial crises that accompany the rising cost of medical science will influence political elections and health care policy for years to come. Unfortunately, given the ongoing pressures to contain costs, the prevention and recovery phases of treatment could be neglected. A logical way to cut costs is to focus on acute care. However, an over emphasis on acute medicine can eclipse the need for psychological and spiritual contributions to a balance of prevention, treatment and recovery.

In an effort to contain costs, the health industry has developed a well-intended strategy of quality assurance and review. This approach of monitoring cost and procedures based on limiting expenditures defined as "usual and customary costs and fees" (DRGs, i.e., diagnostic related groups), has contained some costs. However, this strategy has also created other difficulties. One alarming trend is that acute treatment is becoming the only phase of health care that is reimbursable by insurance carriers. The importance of prevention and recovery is known; the reality is that diagnosis and treatment (the acute phase of disease) receive most of the health dollar.

A related distinction in health care has been the difference between curative and palliative care. Curative connotes procedures or medicines that reverse the course of a syndrome or disease. Palliative connotes procedures or medicines which aid recovery, prevention or rehabilitation but may be the central treatment. However, the two terms are not mutually exclusive, and the separation of the two aspects of care can create problems. Prevention and recovery may be more palliative than curative.

Authorization for payment of medical services considered palliative is generally the first health care budget cost to be eliminated in tight fiscal times. In his recent book, *Medicine at the Crossroads*, Konner (1993) suggests that health care is not healthy and that many sectors are responsible. The U.S. insurance "industry" is a vast bureaucracy encompassing fifteen hundred private businesses. These insurance entities often reach far into the lives of patients. In order to process insurance, information must be passed along to agents of the insurance company. Often this information is a violation of confidentiality. Previously, only reporting a diagnosis was required, which was viewed as a minimal threat to privacy. Recently, however, more confidential and personal information has been required to get treatment "authorized." With this trend, the likelihood of violation of confidentiality becomes real and frightening. This trend is particularly intrusive in mental health treatment. External "treatment police" (case managers, "quality reviewers" or other gatekeepers) are rewarded for reducing costs whenever possible. In principle, this strategy is an important cost counterbalance. In application, the case manager strategy often means that a patient's confidentiality is ethically compromised. This violation of confidentiality can compromise the therapeutic relationship. Konner further explains that insurance companies can at their whim refuse to insure individuals who are sick or who otherwise appear a bad risk. This process has been called *red-lining*. Consequently, people who have paid insurance premiums for years can now be turned out on the street when they get sick. An insurance company can increase its premiums significantly and then offer large discounts to people who have no history of sickness. This practice is called *policy churning*.

Another dimension that contributes to the troublesome state of health care is a malpractice redress system. Less than 2 percent of actual negligent acts by physicians reach the courts or a lawsuit. And on the average, only half of those lead to monetary awards; however, the awards that are made are significant. These large awards may give the impression that this litigation driven process controls physician error or ineptitude. In truth, the vast majority of negligent and mistaken acts are neither detected nor punished. In contrast, a system such as the one in Sweden allows a mechanism for compensating patients who are harmed from treatment. There the system is set up in such a way that doctors can help patients gain redress for errors. This is done independently of the courts. Even though the financial awards are smaller than those usually awarded by the courts in the United States, in Sweden compensation is a cooperative rather than an adversarial process for restitution.

As most observers of the U.S. health system are now aware, one reason for spiraling cost is the physician's need to practice "defensive medicine." A physician feels she must take every possible diagnostic precaution rather than overlook the low probability diagnostic issues. Stated another way, when in doubt extra tests are ordered to make sure that no error is made. Obviously, this drives up the cost of health care. This climate encourages an almost feverish overreliance on technology in order to prevent error. Incidentally, that diagnostic technology is one of the largest components of increased cost in health care.

These are perplexing forces shaping the culture of medicine. Physicians complain that they are no longer in control of the delivery of health care. Sensitive to the consequences of error, they defensively perform extensive procedures to reduce the likelihood of litigation. Insurance companies blame spiraling cost on unnecessary procedures and therefore work to reduce access to these procedures in order to contain costs. And the courts may take the position that inept or haphazard medicine causes this legally threatening atmosphere. More costly health care excludes payment for prevention and increases payment for the acute aspects of treatment, while physicians complain that contradictory cost-cutting imperatives dictate the way they practice.

This current health care system is only one aspect of the culture of medicine. Another area worth noting is the training of physicians. The senior author spent more than fifteen years as faculty in medical school settings. This work included not only training physicians and other health professionals, but also providing psychotherapy for physicians and medical students. One of the most predictable "crises of idealism" occurs when young doctors take the important step from the basic sciences (usually the first two years of medical training) into the clinics or applied clinical experiences (traditionally the last two years of medical school). When these apprentice doctors begin to work in clinical settings, they are shocked by the sheer number of patients who must be seen each day These novice physicians soon learn that wise and caring principles of practice are often compromised by the heavy workload in the real world of medicine.

Long hours and arduous "on call" expectations are part of the initiation into medicine. Based on his personal experience, Konner (1987) describes in a vivid and articulate way how the ordeal of training as a physician shapes the attitudes, endurance and sense of importance that mark the physician's archetypal persona. His accounts are enlightening and we recommend his work, *Becoming a Doctor: A Journey of Initiation in Medical School.* Konner, an anthropologist, who went through medical training in a way similar to how he became part of some other tribes, shares his insights about his personal and professional experience. He tells us that interns and residents are under the greatest pressure they have ever been or ever will be during their clinical and postgraduate training. He describes them as exceedingly overworked and sleep deprived, with huge responsibilities. They are crushed under the medical hierarchy and bewildered by an onslaught of ever-changing technical facts. Moreover, they are at the lowest end of the pecking order. The fledgling or novice physician is inducted into a role whereby the mentor's message is "do as I say, not as I do." The nonverbal message is to do whatever the student feels is right; but if they are to survive they should imitate their mentors. Konner describes how physician's attitudes, moral posture, mind-set and clinical decisions are all shaped by the arduous initiation of internship and residency.

The obvious question that arises is why must the training be this way? Konner sampled the answers and found the following. One "house officer" (the attending physician mentor) described it as slave labor. Interns and residents work on these bizarre and nightmarish schedules so that senior physicians in hospitals can make ends meet or thrive. A second answer offered is that "we had to do it, so you have to do it." According to this theory, the more senior physicians require the novices to go through the terrible stress they did, jump through the same hoops and experience the total ritual or initiation process. The third suggestion, which Konner found more palpable, was one offered by the famed physician, Sir William Osler. Osler suggested that the physician must "live on the wards." In order to become intimate with disease and suffering, he stated you must live close to it and experience every aspect of it. There is an ethic in medical training that the student should gain as much exposure to every clinical experience and disease presentation as possible. This may be one reason why residents do not plead for shorter hours. This stress hardiness is part of the ethic and initiation into the physician culture and value system.

The doctor is inculcated into a posture of emotional detachment. Konner says that at the beginning of his training, he felt that this role induction was an unfortunate side effect of training. However, he came to believe that the attitude was intrinsic. Sometimes medical doctors' aloof attitude is excused because their training and practice schedules are so demanding. Perhaps the best defense against the physician's emotional risks is a dispassionate attitude. While this attitude sometimes draws the ire of nonphysicians, it makes sense from a guild or anthropological perspective.

Konner thinks that most Americans are, so far, unwilling to sacrifice scientific and technical perfection (in which they believe) for more humane or caring medical treatment. Patients may contribute to unidimensional treatment through an exaggerated faith in medical technology.

I call physicians "Healing artisans." Artisans is a word, requiring explanation. Doctors are not scientists, at least not in the medical roles, because though they certainly draw on science, what they do is neither objective nor oriented to the production of new knowledge—nor should it be. And they are certainly not artists, since aesthetic principles and independent creativity have little or no place in practice, despite everything that has been said about the "art" of medicine. The doctors are craftspeople of the highest order. Sometimes like engineers, they lean heavily on science. Sometime like diamond cutters, they seem to be coasting along on pure skill. And occasionally like glass blowers or goldsmiths, what they do verges on art. But in almost all cases doctors are practical, no nonsense women and men who have given their lives to this craft of theirs and do not suffer fools gladly. They are as brilliant, hard working, and dedicated a group as one would find in any profession, and they are more of all three than most. When I talk about what I think is missing I mean accomplishments that would have to be grafted onto an already prodigious set of achievements. I do not want to belittle those achievements when I say that what is missing is at least as important as what is there. (Konner, 1987, p. xvii)

Norman Cousins (1990) has also given us an enlightened layperson's perspective on the human craft of the medical profession. He did much to stress the value of humane communication by physicians as a central ingredient in psychoneuroimmunology and the body-mind mutual influence. Doctors who are caring and effective communicators magnify healing. These qualities need to be as important in medical education as are biochemistry, pathology, anatomy and physiology. Emotions and states of mind make a difference. Iatrogenic problems can be caused by insensitive communication of diagnosis or prognosis by the doctor. The weight of a physician's prognosis can be delivered like a hex or as a challenge. The physician artisan can magnify the magic of science with humane communication (Cousins, 1990, pp. 264–268).

Most health professionals would generally support the idea that health care should consider body, mind and spirit. However, in current hospital practice the percentage of time and money allotted for psychological treatment or for addressing the spiritual dimensions is minimal. Reimbursement for only the most acute treatment is the rule. Psychological and spiritual issues (whether they be cause or correlate of a physical illness) are usually scant considerations in the culture of medicine. There are some reasons for hope, however. Herbert Benson, a physician and professor at Harvard Medical School and Beth Israel Hospital, has consistently proposed a more integrated approach to health care. He has been involved in an extensive research program clarifying the impact of psychological and spiritual factors on health (Benson, 1975, 1984, 1987 and 1996). His more recent works have focused on the role of spirituality and faith in impacting health. Benson continues a tradition of scholarly research that incorporates and integrates mind, body and spirit.

Blazer (1991) is another excellent example of a physician who has incorporated the psychological and spiritual components into his framework for healing. His efforts have been specifically geared to integrating these dimensions in his work with the aging. Callahan (1995) has stressed that priorities and limits on health spending must be reconsidered and rebalanced. We cannot pay for everything we want, yet we may leave out essential aspects of care if treatment ignores principles of prevention and well advised rehabilitation. Many voices would argue that medicine needs psyche and soul as well as soma if it is indeed going to be "healthy" health care. Otherwise this refection by Updike could come true.

In my embarrassment I wandered off and pondered the marvelous devices offered in this medical center for the use and easement of old age; canes and braces and pans and wheel-chairs, and toilet seats thickened like a club foot's

shoe, and long cane-like pincers to retrieve what can no longer be bent over for: a veritable armory as complex as a medieval knight's own grail. Now simply the indefinite prolongation of life.
—John Updike [Reflections while waiting for his aging mother as she is examined in the hospital]

Cultures of Psychology: Aspirations and Realities

Listen, or your tongue will make you deaf.
—Native American saying

The culture of psychology strives for a clearer identity. There is an amazing array of mental health professions and disciplines (and some would say undisciplines). There are several paths to become a physician of the psyche. The field encompasses the clinical and counseling psychologist, psychiatrist, mental health counselor, clinical social worker, psychiatric nurse practitioner, marriage and family therapist, pastoral counselor and others. This spectrum of therapists may create uncertainty, confusion or bewilderment in potential clients.

For example, the profession of clinical psychology has struggled with some success in gaining recognition alongside America's medical culture. The authors are most sensitive to these struggles. The following story is a funny example of the quest for identity. After World War II in the United States, a more visible profession of clinical psychology began to emerge. Psychologists' identity evolved as researchers (in both healthy and abnormal psychology) and as craftsmen applying scientific principles to understanding and treating psychological disorders. A colleague, Willis McCann, shared this interesting anecdote about the emergence of psychology as a profession. McCann's doctoral degree (Ph.D.) was actually in abnormal psychology from the University of Indiana before there was a distinct profession of clinical psychology. Dr. McCann had been an officer in the United States Army on the strength of his military infantry training rather than his earned doctorate. He was asked to serve on an Army task force to recommend where a profession of psychology should fit in the hierarchy of medical service in the Army's bureaucracy. McCann served on this committee and tried to clarify to the Army's officials the difference between clinical psychology and psychiatry. Guided more by the questioning of the bureaucrats than his own preferred way of explaining the distinction, McCann was asked if clinical psychology dealt with *sanity* as well as *insanity*. He cautiously agreed to this distinction hoping that it would allow psychologists in the military to offer a broad spectrum of clinical health services. After many interviews and recommendations, McCann and his colleagues eagerly awaited the results of the special panel. He gasped his surprise when they received the blue ribbon panel's decision. They made the recommendation that clinical psychology should be placed in the *Sanitation Corps* of the military's chain of command. Back to the drawing board!

Observers of current services and professions in the area of psychological diagnosis and treatment know that amazing battles have taken place and continue to rage between the medical camp (psychiatrists) and the psychologist camp. There is a history of federal antitrust suits filed and won to ensure psychology's independent practice from the supervision of physicians. Regardless of one's allegiance in these wars, it is clearly an ongoing struggle for legitimacy. Unfortunately guild issues waste and divert creative resources that could instead be used to enhance a health care that is wise in the ways of mind-body interaction.

Psychology has its own identity and wisdom, yet struggles to find its place in that spectrum. Clearly, there is a fiscal and financial advantage to being a profession allied with the medical model in Western cultures. The aura of medicine lends legitimacy and some protection (albeit tenuous) within the biomedical guild. Psychotherapists' culture could simply imitate medical doctors. On the other hand, there is value in a separate culture, or guild, for the physician of the psyche. The psychologist Perry London (1986) suggests that psychotherapists represent the "secular priesthood." Psychological physicians offer alternative answers to spiritual questions for those who do not embrace a traditional religion. This introduction to the guild and cultures of psychological treatment is meant to convey the need for the still evolving state of the culture of psychology.

Charles Kiesler (1992), a former president of the American Psychological Association, wrote an interesting article, "U.S. Mental Health Policy: Doomed to Fail." He argues that if psychology merely imitates the structure and agenda of American medicine, we may do ourselves and our patients (or clients) a disservice. The needs of the psyche may be wrongly distorted to fit a medical model. The result could preclude the best plan for psychological prevention and treatment.   Mental health care must be tailored to human psychological needs rather than simply medical reimbursement rules. Psychology has created an influential perspective of science, art and craft. Strength emerges from the struggle to present this wisdom integrated with the other cultures.

We offer the following suggestion. Viktor Frankl in the quote (cited at the start of this chapter) urged a balance of body, mind and spirit. Determining which of these three faces of psychology is most visible at any one time depends largely on the context of treatment, the kinds of patients/clients treated and the training of the treatment provider. An analogy may help clarify the dimensions of psychology from a more medical/health psychology focus to a more traditional clinical/counseling focus to a more existential/humanistic focus.

A useful way to grasp the three facets of psychological care is to think of three corresponding rooms. The *first* is a medical room of psychological treatment. In a medical context or setting, these physicians of the psyche are expected to wear the white coat "uniform." Practitioners here often work with a variety of physicians (i.e., neurologists, oncologists, etc.) in addressing psychological issues in persons with medical or health-related disorders. The language and procedures used here often create a more medically focused context and ambiance. A *second* room for the therapist is the more traditional office setting. Apparently, the Freudian tradition set the tone of a comfortable (if not curious) furnished office with desk, couch, easy chairs and the archetypal books and diplomas—all the trappings of academic and scientific legitimacy. Most of the outpatient work in the United States is a variation of this traditional office setting. The traditional culture of psychological treatment has its own room. A *third* room of psychological treatment might be described as the existential/humanistic room. This could conjure images of a more Eastern influence with a high degree of focus on questions of meaning, responsibility, and so on. However, existential rooms can also exist in more traditional pastoral counseling settings such as churches and synagogues.

Perhaps this metaphor of three rooms helps capture psychology's role options. We find the rooms a useful analogy in training psychologists and other stripes of psychotherapists. The distinction can help the provider make informed decisions about which treatments and approaches will best address the needs of the patient/client. The three rooms also suggest ways the culture of psychology may join with medical and spiritual cultures, better integrating the three dimensions. The culture of psychology can have a wise and independent identity without being excluded from the power of the business and culture of medicine. Psychology has its own legacy of wisdom and treatment.

> Everything that irritates us about others can lead us to an understanding of ourselves.
> —Carl Jung

> Therapy is indeed a limited arrangement: a relative degree of power is provisionally designated in a restricted context for a circumscribed period of time. But even this somewhat makeshift arrangement would be nothing but sham *if the therapist were not an expert*—that is a repository of informed uncertainty—about the human condition, individual and family development, processes of psychological change, and the handling of dialogue, metaphors and stories.
> —Salvador Minuchin

> No one can afford to give up any part of themselves. All of you is worth something. Even the evil can be a source of vitality if only you can face it and transform it.
> —Sheldon Kopp, *If You Meet the Buddha on the Road, Kill Him*

> One should learn to listen with an intensity most people save for talking.
> —Lily Tomlin

Psychology looms as the best candidate to understand, illuminate and influence mind-body interactions. Psychology also offers crucial strategies to heal and enhance relationships in communities, families, friends and lovers. Psychology's main dilemma however, may be deciding where it will settle in the landscape of health and healing for seniors. Will psychology evolve as a health guild in the business of medicine? Will psychology become the "secular priesthood?" Or can psychology develop an integrated culture of its own? Psychotherapy offers older adults a place to tell, revise and make sense of their life stories. Psychotherapy offers a science of emotion and the balm of a genuinely caring human relation.

Cultures of Religion and Spirituality: Grace, Meaning and Ethic (Aspirations and Realities)

Parting is all we know of heaven and all we need of hell.
—Emily Dickinson

Through the ages, spiritual and religious quests have blessed (at their best) and cursed (at their misguided worst) humanity's progress. Now the spiritual horizon stretches from orthodox traditions through "reformed" options to free-form spiritual communions, all the way to agnostic and atheistic angst. Spiritual/religious cultures offer us a conviction, a struggle of the soul, an ethic and a comfort. Tillich's quote (below) about grace conveys much about a spiritual need. Spirituality is known to magnify healing forces, to comfort in the face of sickness and death and to create a community of direction, support, activism and fellowship. Religion and spirituality are often intertwined and absorbed in ethnic, racial and tribal cultures, just as medicine and psychology are nested in their guilds, tribes or business landscapes.

Spiritual contributions to meaning, and the ethics of health and healing with older adults, are vital and varied. If depression and demoralization are the cohort of sickness and loss, then hope and healing are the gift of religious peace. Religious traditions through the centuries have produced inspiring metaphors of renewal and growth, of meaning and comfort, of focus and higher power.

Religion is also capable of ghastly misdirection such as "holy wars" and racial religious purges, or spiritual beliefs that are psychologically harmful. However, a litany of these errors is not our focus here.

My karma ran over your dogma.
—Anonymous

I am determined my children shall be brought up in their father's religion, if they can find out what it is.
—Charles Lamb

The inability to articulate clearly the sense of spiritual integration should not be taken as sign of its absence.
—S. McFadden and R. Gerl (1990)

The largest part of helping is to give courage.
—Irish proverb

Grace strikes us when we are in great pain and restlessness
it strikes us when our disgust for our own being, our weakness, our hostility, and our lack of direction and composure
have become intolerable to us. It strikes us when, year after
year, the longed for perfection of life does not appear, when
old compulsions reign with us as they have for decades.
Sometimes at that moment a wave of light breaks into our
darkness, and it is as though a voice were saying, "you are
accepted."
—Paul Tillich, *The Shaking of the Foundations*

The ethical meaning of religious metaphors (like sacrament
and covenant) would be a welcome influence on managed health care's
contrasting metaphors of cost-containment and "preauthorization." The
business of health care has different saints and different sinners than
other religions.

Building on the idea of healing metaphors, healing stories and
healing beliefs, let us consider some of the varied yet powerful offerings the spiritual dimension provides. Spirituality represents a meaning
before, during and after other meanings such as medicine or psychology
fail. Hall (1985) considers spirituality and its expression to be a
creative force that helps transcend the crises of life's stages. This force
or perspective can provide meaning across crisis, tragedies and generations.

Old Time Religion

Flannery O'Connor is an excellent storyteller about old time
religion. She has an idiosyncratic moral imagination that is both tragic
and hopeful at the same time. Hers is not an easy "row to hoe." She is
suspicious of intellectuals far removed from the grief and glory of everyday life. She quotes Pascal and seriously applies his advice. One
should believe in "the God of Abraham, Isaac and Jacob and not of the
philosophers and scholars." She champions the relentless virtues of the
South and did so even when the rest of the country attacked its moral
and political stubbornness. What she loved about her southern homeland included this strong religious tradition, the sobering experience of

defeat and violation producing a tragic sensibility. O'Connor also had "a distrust of the abstract, a sense of dependence on the grace of god, and a knowledge that evil is not simply a problem to be solved, but a mystery to be endured." (Coles, 1993, pp. xiv, 112).

O'Connor emphasized that the meaning of the story should go on expanding for the reader the more he or she thinks about it. Meaning, however, cannot be captured in an interpretation. O'Connor once reproached an English professor who attempted to have his students explain her work. She accused the professor and his ninety students of "creating something fantastic and completely removed" from her intentions. She allowed that if it were an accurate interpretation the story would be little more than a trick and its interest would simply be for abnormal psychology, something she was not interested in contributing to. Her sentiments here are consistent with Eastern religions' emphasis on the direct experiencing of and apprehending of meaning and truth versus an experience of meaning that relies on verbalizations and analysis. If teachers are in the habit of approaching a story as if were a research problem where any answer is believable, then students will never learn to enjoy fiction. Too much interpretation is certainly worse than too little.

Another example of a more traditional religious viewpoint is one offered by Brinton (1969). In his history of Quakerism, he argues that at any point in the life of an organized religious group there will be one of four prominent areas of interest or effort: (1) a mystical or inward, spiritually focused emphasis; (2) an evangelical or outwardly focused emphasis; (3) a theological or rationally focused emphasis; or (4) an activistic or socially focused emphasis. Although he applies this understanding to religious movements, it appears that this framework might also lead to an increased understanding of an individual's spiritual journey. For the individual, one or more of these emphasis areas will be more prominent and meaningful at some points and less so at others. It follows that one or more of these areas will take on increased importance for an individual as he or she ages. The concept contributes to a person's view of the spiritual dimension.

Sampling other cultural and religious traditions, the European Jewish community (before its decimation in World War II) produced spiritual and literary treasures. In addition to Sholom Aleichem and Isaac Bashevis Singer, perhaps the Jewish storytellers best known to Americans, Elie Weisel has written at length in an attempt to capture the oral tradition of learning by story and legend. In *Gates of the Forest*, Weisel (1966) conveys an optimism despite misfortune and even horror.

> There is joy as well as fury in the hasid's dancing. It's his way of proclaiming. "You don't want me to dance? Too bad, I'll dance anyhow." You've taken away every reason for singing, but I shall sing. You didn't expect my joy, but here it is; yes, my joy will rise up; it will submerge you. (p. 196)

Sholom Aleichem's Yiddish stories convey an optimism told over and over through tales of misfortune. In the introduction to a collection of Aleichem's stories, Alfred Kazin commented that "One of the things you get from Sholom Aleichem is this mockery of language, a mockery which carries a boundless pleasure in language and a sense of the positive strength that goes with mighty talk" (Kazin, 1956, p. xii). In his short stories of Tevye the dairy man (later transformed into the play *Fiddler on the Roof*), Aleichem's characters themselves make this point. Tevye muses, "What can I say to her? Most fathers would scold a child for such talk, punish her, even beat her maybe. But Tevye is not a fool. To my way of thinking anger doesn't get you anywhere. So I tell her a story I speak to her half in fun and half in anger, and all the time my heart weeps. But Tevye is no weakling; I control myself" (Kazin, 1956, p. 398). Thus, "in Jewish humor, [the self] laughs at itself—the explanation for this presumably being that among a people with so long a history of persecution, the most pressing task of humor has been to neutralize the hostility of the outside world, first by internalizing it and then by detonating it through a joke" (Aleichem, 1987, pp. xv–xvi). This certainly is a spiritual/cultural example of the psychological notion of learned optimism.

> No one else must ever know what I'm about to tell you.
> We all need to confide in someone. If no one knows your
> secret, it's not a secret but just a hidden thing.
> —Isaac Bashevis Singer, *A Crown of Feathers*
> (p. 213)

From the same Jewish tradition, Martin Buber's (1958, 1995) writings, aphorisms, teachings and revival of the mystical movement of Hasidism create a model for the divine possibilities of human relationships. Buber is probably best known for highlighting the magic of relationships he called "I-Thou" relations. These are marked by a transcendent caring for one another which is inspired by one's relationship with a divine deity. The I-Thou relation is also often held as a model for the way a psychotherapy relation helps the healing process.

The following brief aphorisms give a sampling of his thoughtful inspiration (Buber, 1995).

> From the child you can learn three things
> He is merry for no particular reason;
> Never for a moment is he idle;
> When he needs something, he
> demands it vigorously. (p. 55)

> Dreams are a secretion of our thoughts and through them our thought is purified. All the wisdom in the world is a secretion of the Torah, and through it the Torah is purified. (p. 60)

> For the unlearned old age is winter; for the learned it is the season of harvest.
> —The Talmud

> All suffering prepares the soul for vision.
> —Martin Buber

In addition to the specific content of belief, the rituals and liturgies that religions offer provide a "map of the territory" of comfort. These rituals can celebrate and mark life's developmental progression and make sense of the changes that accompany aging and death.

Prest and Keller (1993) are psychotherapists who do a nice job of incorporating both traditional and nontraditional religious emphases into their work with families. They offer models and strategies to use spiritual beliefs and metaphors in family therapy. Knowing and honoring senior's religious values, strengthens medical and psychological forces in health and healing.

Emerging Spirituality

Religious doctrine serves as a defense against religious experience.
　　　　　—Joseph Campbell

Spiritual life is to learn how to stop running away from things we don't like and face the whole of our life—birth and death—and to live here now with what *Zorba the Greek* called "the whole catastrophe," with your heart open. It is being open to the mystery of not knowing.
　　　　　—Jack Kornfeld

For some people religion is a coat that does not fit. The nature lovers' spirituality is a joy and renewal that comes from interacting with the environment, cultivating the ocean and the earth, growing things and merely admiring and preserving nature. The benefit is a generative source of power beyond ourselves. These folks might eschew religion but accept a spiritual label. Similarly, art in many forms is a source of knowledge, challenge and renewal. The audience, artist and critic of art are all members of that metaphorical church: art (literature, music, painting, theater, cinema, etc.) can be a source of abundant possibilities, inspiration and eternal meaning. Art can provoke, wound, inform and inspire.

There is a growing body of what may be called nontraditional spirituality. On the one hand, this is a new direction, and on the other hand, it is one of the oldest traditions in recorded civilization. In order to make some sense of this approach to spirituality, we will use the recent works of Joan Borysenko, including *Minding the Body, Mending the Mind* to give further clarity. Borysenko is a research cell biologist retrained in psychology who is now exploring practical aspects of spirituality. The other writer we will mention here traces a viable option for understanding and applying nontraditional spirituality. Thomas Moore's book, *Care of the Soul,* points to valuable directions for healthy spirituality throughout the stages of life.

To understand these efforts, it is helpful to reflect on the meaning of spirituality. McFadden and Gerl (1990) consider spirituality the central integrative process people use to make sense of their relationship to themselves, others, nature and powers that transcend the individual. Payne (1990) also considers spirituality to be primarily an integrative and synthesizing force. Given this view, one can see that while for many people traditional religions satisfactorily serve this function, for others they do not.

Borysenko's working definition of spirituality includes a sense of connectedness with self, with others and with a greater source. She makes a distinction between spirituality and religion, although the two are not necessarily separate. Dr. Borysenko's research reveals that a prime buffer against stress is a sense of purpose, meaning and social support. These points appear consistent with similar arguments by Benson (1996).

In the area of *personal connectedness,* Borysenko draws from psychological research, which points out that a "false self" or an inauthentic self creates a dissonance and cuts us off from personal power. Traditional religion calls this sin. If we act in a way that is not true to our values, our highest potential and a sense of fidelity, we tear ourselves off from this important strength. A second area is *connectedness with others.* Lack of trust and intimacy (building on the need for personal fidelity) can interfere with friendship. The third dimension is *connectedness with a greater source* (or what she calls a transpersonal dimension). This builds on the concept of a world view. Is the universe a friendly place or not? The answer to this question is a potential source of strength. Those people whose world views are characterized by religious guilt or spiritual pessimism find themselves cut off from a natural order or source of unity and strength. While this concept may seem foreign to some, she anchors the importance of one's world view in Martin Seligman's research (cited earlier) on learned optimism and learned helplessness. People's beliefs in greater power, sources of renewal and an ability to shape destiny can provide both comfort and strength.

Reframing our experience puts our life, our daily tasks and our styles of relatedness in perspective. Borysenko shares a traditional anecdote about a stranger who asks three brick masons what they are doing. One mason answers that he is "jerking these lame bricks from one place to another." The second mason says that he is "making a living." A third mason explains that he is "building a cathedral." A world view that reflects a greater purpose than ourselves can produce *stress hardiness,* or a reason to endure hardship for a higher good.

Some research on heart attacks suggests that they often happen on Monday morning as a result of "joyless striving." The prospect of returning to meaningless work or a joyless striving may kill the spirit.

A research program pursued by Suzanne Kobasa and her colleagues (i.e., Kobasa, 1979; Kobasa, Maddi and Kahn, 1982) traces the qualities that predict a hardiness which buffers people from the effect of high stress and multiple life changes. These qualities describe a person who is an active and a responsible creator, one who thrives on change and challenge and is able to make courageous commitments. These people have a clear sense of purpose and involvement with others. They are able to incorporate events into a chosen life plan, and they view change as a positive experience. Even the Type A competitive personality (originally found to predict a higher risk for heart disease) may not lead to higher health risks. If the competitive Type A person is driven by optimistic commitment rather than hostile competition, the future for health and happiness is much brighter.

In developing a concept of stress hardiness, Borysenko draws on Kobasa's work. She identifies the three C's of hardiness: challenge, control and commitment. Denying the challenge or finding it a tedious adversary is not as effective as the posture of the fighter who realizes that a challenge can be strengthening. In the area of control, the research on learned helplessness or learned optimism (Seligman, 1991) suggests that our perception of how much we influence our fate can strengthen our stress hardiness. The third "C," commitment, draws heavily on Viktor Frankl's work. Frankl notes that a sudden loss of hope and courage can have a deadly effect on the immune system and our physical well-being. In *The Doctor and the Soul,* he suggests that we can create a meaning in life by the way we relate to others and by the goals and endeavors with which we plot our life course.

Thomas Moore (1992, 1996), a Jungian analyst who lived as a monk in a Catholic monastery for twelve years, describes ways to find sacredness in everyday life and suggests important directions to consider. Other religious traditions also highlight this possibility. One of the fundamental tenets of Quakerism, for example is that there is no distinction between the sacred and secular. This viewpoint considers all of life to be sacred (Cooper, 1990). The first point Moore makes is that we can see the sacred in the ordinary. He suggests, for example, compiling a memory box of thoughts, experiences or pictures that have meaning for our past and direction for our future. Second, he suggests "growing old is one of the ways the soul nudges itself (to attend to) the spiritual aspect of life." Age forces us to decide what is important in life. Energy spent to work against a natural process can steer us away from spiritual strength. Moore cautions that church-going in some cases could be a psychological defense against the power of the "holy," but daily meditation and refocus on a treasured belief is a source of strength. A third suggestion is that dreams and aspirations are a person's own mythology and imagery a source of guidance. Myth, he says, sometimes has a connotation of falsehood ("only a myth"). Myth may seem a flight of fancy, but its fantastic imagery takes us away from life's too burdensome and realistic details and can inspire extraordinary accomplishments. The myth can inspire extraordinary accomplishments. A story of majesty and comfort renews the spirit.

Renewal is a powerful spiritual value across religions and across cultures. Moore describes volumes of literature on the "rivers of change" and other metaphors for renewal. The concept of grace (see the quote by Tillich earlier in this chapter) captures the need and value of renewal in the face of guilt, demoralization and depression.

Relatedness is another theme in a healthy spirituality. We can only treat badly those whose souls we disregard or ignore. In creativity and beauty there is a reanimation of life. In mythology the soul of youth is the *puer* quality. Moore says that the *puer* spirit is also essential for healthy aging. The energy and innocence of youth can be deepened by integrity, relatedness and renewal in the face of life's losses and challenges. *Reanimation* and renewal come from connecting with forces stronger or more enduring than ourselves.

An additional strength in everyday spirituality comes from knowing and making peace with the darker side of living. The dark, the weak, the evil and the tragic all are challenges to character. Knowledge of the Jungian concept of the shadow fosters grace and renewal. Mastery comes from facing, absorbing and transcending the tragic. In some cases, death itself is a form of growth and healing from a spiritual perspective.

Consider this irony about the evolution of medicine from religion. Joseph Campbell, who wrote widely on mythology and culture, traced the relation between dogma, architecture and spiritual values from the dark ages to the present. Campbell traced the fascinating trajectory of spiritual universals and religious beliefs. In his presentation, he showed how the architecture of healing evolved from the Catholic

Church and into the medical hospital. He showed how the gothic architecture of vaulted cathedrals and stations of the cross (alongside the center aisles leading to the altar) evolved as churches became hospitals. In this transition, the stations of the cross became patient beds. The center aisle still led to the altar—now the doctors/nurses station. The Holy evolved from God to doctors! In this architectural and ideological evolution, Campbell showed how hospitals emerged with center hallways flanked by treatment beds bordering the center aisle. Medical icons became the altar of this new "religion." The three cultures (body, mind and spirit) are part of one effort. Which is the most holy?

> He is an Episcopalian, an agnostic, an anythingarian seeking to overthrow our holy faith.
> —James Joyce, *Ulysses* (p. 490)

The need for a nontraditional spiritual expression does not always come from outside the established religious framework. Robinson (1963), an Anglican scholar, provides an excellent review of Dietrich's Bonhoeffer's ideal of "religionless Christianity." Bonhoeffer focused on the idea of religion as being concerned with the mechanisms for navigating church ritual and structures, whereas spirituality focused more on the broader concept of finding meaning in one's life. "Religion" may or may not be helpful in the spiritual quest. Knowing that thoughts such as these were being expressed fifty years ago by a Lutheran clergyman may help traditionally focused religious people become more comfortable with nontraditional approaches.

Universal Spiritual Principles

Blazer (1991) suggests six dimensions which he believes comprise spiritual well-being. He suggests universal principles to enlighten and improve the treatment of seniors. The first of these principles is *self-determined wisdom*. This component involves acceptance of the limits present in life. Although acceptance does not prevent reasonable change to the environment, it does prevent one from trying to upset the balance of nature and the natural system. The second component is *self-transcendence*. This occurs when a person can cross a boundary beyond the self, give up some of the illusions of life and have greater openness to life as it is. The third component is *meaning*. A spiritual approach can assist the elder in making sense out of existence and provide hope for the present moment. The fourth component is *accepting the totality of life*. This factor echoes Erikson's eighth stage of development (Integrity versus Despair). The fifth component is the *revival of spirituality*. One can see new vitality in activities that bring both personal satisfaction and social usefulness. Blazer argues that advocacy for the aged is a valuable task that helps create this legacy for many elders. The sixth dimension is exit and *existence*. The focus here is to see death not as a failure (by either the individual or the health care system) but rather as a step in the developmental process which can be memorialized with rituals. Such honoring rituals sustain life and meaning across the generations.

> I came that you may have life and have it more abundantly.
> —Jesus of Nazareth

The cultures of religion or spirituality, just like the cultures of medicine and psychology, are haunted by human idiosyncrasies as well as motives of greed and power. Nevertheless, it is clear that the cultures of spirituality provide invaluable support and direction in a quest for health and healthy aging. These cultures can suggest universal principles. The first is a sense of meaning and purpose. Related to that principle is the creation of an ethic or a wisdom about the healthiest ways to relate, to have a guiding morality. Another principle understood well by religious options is human limitation. Some religions might call this sin, while some spiritual dimensions might call this duplicity or human frailty. Limitations should not be celebrated; however, a valuable spiritual belief offers a way to accept limitations and yet continue on a life path. Consequently, some concept of grace or forgiveness seems to be imperative in allowing humans to recognize shortcomings but not be weighted down by their faults, thus blocking future growth or selfacceptance. Paul Tillich's words on grace earlier in this chapter capture this concept well. Grace is related to renewal or transformation. This concept runs through religions across the ages and across cultures. Culture stories and bible stories alike convey messages of setting aside an old form and creating a new one. It is important to stress that the religious concepts of renewal and transformation are entirely consistent with the healthy psychological and physical principles that we have described throughout this book. The concept of renewal is a variation on the theme of balancing change and continuity. Renewal is a reworking of old ways of being, a creation of vital and abundant possibilities. The last principle is hope. Hope may spring from meaning, from purpose, from ethic, from grace or from renewal. For older adults the prospect of life ending may dampen hope. Despair is our fate without a sense of continuity, a lasting value or lineage (generativity). Physical and psychological dimensions of health desperately need the benefits of an ethic or spirituality that bestows lasting meaning, renewal and hope.

A Tale of Three Cultures: Harmony and Dissonance

Each of the cultures has advantages and drawbacks. Blending the cultures of mind, body and spirit, yet preserving each one's special value, is a healthy and healing aspiration. An important way to blend the cultures is to fully appreciate a spectrum of *curative, palliative* and *rehabilitative* aspects of health and healing.

In an important article, "Old Age, Rehabilitation and Research: A Review of the Issues," Becker and Kaufman (1988) explain that negative societal values about aging adversely affect medical decisions about treating seniors. Low expectations of how well older people can function after illness can lead to rationing the rehabilitation health services older people receive. Rehabilitation may fall in the palliative rather than curative category of medicine in the minds of ageist administrators or health professionals. The purpose of Medicare, the U.S. government health insurance for elderly enacted in 1985, is to provide treatment for acute curative illness episodes. Medicare does not, nor did it ever, provide for extended rehabilitative or long-term care. Judicious rehabilitative efforts (as valuable as acute treatment) can reduce future medical utilization. Also, emotional support from family and friends helps promote the patient's optimal response to medical treatment.

We hope this book serves to provoke health professionals, caregivers and families to locate and create places where body, mind and spirit are all truly valued in treatment. Continuity of care is important. *Continuity of care* and *aging in place* are the highest aspiration current health systems struggle mightily to be financially viable. The ethics of treatment must guide rather than be led by profit motives. Healthy models of treatment are available. The three cultures could compete with or ignore each other. The three cultures in balance can provide the most healthy and meaningful third stage of life. Figure 1 below is a Venn diagram of how the three cultures may complement each other. Continuity of care and health should extend across the three cultures. Committed caregivers in each culture can foster that goal. Principles of health and places where healthy treatment exists are traced in the next chapter.

Figure 1
Interrelation of the Three Cultures

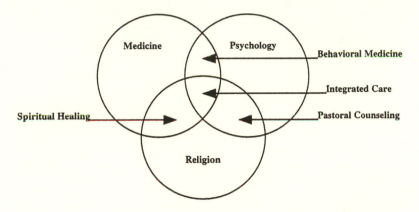

NOTE

Kelly L. Blair, Psy.D. is a psychologist at Whitaker Rehabilitation Center, Winston Salem, North Carolina.

3

Healthy Models: Principles and Places

> Life is what happens to you when you're planning something else.
> —John Lennon

Healthy models for older adults, as for all of us, involve growth, loss, healing and meaning. Places where body, mind and spirit are equally valued are the best places to live, heal, love and grow. Healthy models of development in psychosocial and spiritual dimensions evolve out of the complementary processes of continuity and change. Continuity and change is a deceptively simple summary of an extremely complex way to grow. The continuity dimension refers to the fact that a person, family or community needs to have meaning and identity in order to feel a sense of stability and safety. However, when an identity is never modified and is clung to out of a sense of desperation, creativity and growth may be the victim. Judith Viorst (1986) has written an eloquent book called *Necessary Losses*. Her premise, well founded in clinical research, is that losses, disappointments and surprises can be a challenge to grow through change while still retaining a sense of continuity. Strength of character can come from overcoming challenges and surprises in life.

Probably the most widely accepted model of continuity and change across the lifespan is that of Erik Erikson (and modified by Carol Gilligan, 1983). This eight-stage model of predictable challenges at different periods in life helps us comprehend some of the universal puzzles that all humans face. At each stage in this theory of development, Erikson describes the psychosocial challenge, crisis or dilemma. Gilligan has suggested that Erikson's scheme may be biased in its underappreciation of some essential differences in the developmental demands that women face in contrast to men. A grasp of these predictable stages can provide comfort in knowing that our struggles are shared with others and may be understood in a way that gives hope and actually promotes growth throughout the lifespan.

Erikson's eight stages of development (1982) provide a focus and an aspiration for psychosocial health at each life stage. These stages are:

HOPE (basic trust vs. mistrust)
WILL (autonomy vs. shame)
PURPOSE (initiative vs. guilt)
COMPETENCE (industry vs. inferiority)
FIDELITY (identity vs. identity confusion)
LOVE (intimacy vs. isolation)
CARE (generativity vs. stagnation)
WISDOM (integrity vs. despair/disgust)

Emotional health and psychosocial well-being emerge as a byproduct of resolving the challenges of each age. Sometimes these issues are referred to as developmental crises. The needs at each stage of life continue to reappear throughout life. The idea, however, is that if we have developed some sense of resolution or sense of comfort about those needs, then later life issues are easier to manage. Relative success at earlier developmental times frees us to have more energy for challenges later in life.

Gilligan's cautions about Erikson's model give us a better understanding of the differences between men and women. Erikson's model places a heavy emphasis on identity and achievement as a way of pursuing integrity. Gilligan points out that men are probably more socialized to establish values around integrity and achievement, while women are more socialized to value caring and relatedness earlier in development. Not surprisingly, then, in midlife and later, men may be less prepared to deal with issues of relatedness, intimacy and the value of love. In contrast, women (earlier in life) have learned to value relatedness more than achievement. Consequently, in mid- to later adulthood, it is common for women, having mastered relatedness, to focus on achievement while men, having pursued identity through achievements, need to focus on relatedness and intimacy. We often counsel older couples whose problems center on this paradox; women's needs for relatedness, then achievement, is the opposite development sequence from men's need for achievement, then relatedness.

It is widely recognized that poor experiences in the earliest developmental stages (which focus on trust, autonomy, initiative and industry) can create havoc in later life. Particularly where basic trust has not been established early, an individual may be haunted throughout life by trying to gain that sense of safety. The secret to navigating these life challenges seems rooted in a safe love that launches confidence in later life. Development is affected by wounds that haunt us if they are not addressed. When unencumbered, we can fly into our mature years with hope and purpose. It is said that parents should give their children both roots and wings. Erikson and Gilligan agree that trust, purpose, intimacy and integrity are important for these roots and wings.

There are also predictable stages in a family's life cycle and even across the generations of family. These models share the principle that predictable family challenges create strength through struggle. The strengths gained from these crises or losses can produce a hard-won confidence. Earlier, we called this confidence *expecting well* or *learned optimism*.

This developmental model is a kinder and more hopeful perspective than psychiatric classifications of pathology. The model frames lifespan growth as a task of successfully meeting and resolving challenges. When a person has difficulty moving forward, this may be understood as holding on to an older solution or being stumped by an earlier puzzle. Often the availability of a caring listener, a supportive family or a person who has dealt with a similar dilemma affords the strength and support that lead to creative resolution and hope for the future. Consideration of these human issues and possibilities makes the journey worthwhile.

CONTINUITY AND CHANGE

Health is a balance of life's possibilities and life's struggles. We can help people navigate life's surprises and challenges. There are times when we are overwhelmed; this may be due to the absence of support or stability. We may have encountered losses or dilemmas that leave us feeling despair or stagnation. We may cling to an earlier sense of self that perhaps impedes our continued growth. The ability to reconsider what is valuable and meaningful to us allows health and hope through renewal. Continuity and change can be brought into balance. A family or individual can keep a sense of identity and still change. A life story can be improved while preserving a sense of identity, hope and integrity.

Providing a place that fosters a balance of continuity and change is crucial in promoting and preserving health. One of the factors that keeps health care from being healthy is the lack of continuity in treatment. Consequently, some consideration for healthy models of balanced treatment follow. A rallying cry for healthy aging these days is the concept of "aging in place." This principle simply suggests that in the face of myriad changes and losses, it only makes sense to minimize the number of unwanted moves or changes. Consider the following section on continuity of care. This is followed by a look at places where balance exists. Finally, creating an attitude and environment where no ageism exists will also promote healthy aging.

Continuity of Care

In health care, *prevention, treatment* and *recovery* are equally important. The medical dimension of health should provide all three phases. In reality, the cost of health care has forced an overfocus on the treatment and diagnostic phase of physical health care. Only a token part of the health care dollar goes to prevention and recovery. A healthy model needs a healthy balance of the three phases prevention, treatment and recovery; and of the three dimensions body, mind, and spirit.

Psychology has much to offer in the prevention and recovery phases of illness as well as in the treatment of older adults. Psychology can treat "pure" emotional difficulties as well as the emotional results of physical illness. Psychology can also improve the recovery and healing phase. Nonetheless, psychology has its limits. Much of the culture of psychology, as mentioned earlier, is based on a strong conviction (if not religion) that we can shape our own fate. Generally, that seems true. However, when life's tragedies limit self-determination, we must struggle with difficult questions and dilemmas about the meaning in life. Purpose and meaning in life are important in psychology, but some of life's questions are better answered when informed by religious or spiritual beliefs. Spiritual values complement psychology and help in the prevention and recovery phase as well as acute treatment.

Places of Balance

Some important questions arise in allocating health resources. What do we need and what can we pay for? (Callahan, 1995). What must we keep and what can we live without? How can the cultures of mind, body and spirit work together to help and not hinder health for older adults and their families? Daniel Callahan wrote an important book *(Setting Limits)* about the tough decisions that need to be made. These decisions involve the cost of developing scientific technology and the need to preserve ethical care for older adults and to balance priorities with limited resources.

In this chapter, we will describe some places where medicine, psychology and religion work in an integrated way to help people through their life journey. We also hope to hear from readers about places known to them which integrate the fabric of healing (Friedan, 1993). Sometimes health care actually harm health. Mind and spirit may need to help heal the medical dimension in health care.

Some of the places that we will consider include *hospices, home health care, memory clinics, ecumenical pastoral counseling services, the Elderhostel, and religious community centers,* to name a few.

The Hospice

Hospice is not for mere hand-holding but has been described as "hard medicine with a human face" (by Dame Cicely Saunders a trail blazer in British hospice care). Dame Saunders brought her nursing, social work and medical skills to the creation of appropriate humane and informed care for people with terminal illness. Their families and community can continue with love and support for them through and beyond death.

Sandel Stoddard (1992), in her book, *The Hospice Movement: A Better Way of Caring for the Dying*, describes how the hospice movement has emerged blending the best of British and American models of care. The Hospice at its best weds medicine, religion and psychology. The National Health Service in the United Kingdom supported hospice development in concert with the efforts of, for instance, Dr. F. R. Gusterson. "Dr. Gus was a devout religious man with a twinkle in his eye who believed that hospice work itself was a form of worship" or stewardship (Stoddard, 1992, pp. 228–229). Gusterson felt that the religious dimension should be subtle and low-key, and that professionals must give care and love. "Where we get the strength to do this is our own affair." The hospice is a blend of spirituality, psychology and hard medicine.

Stoddard hopes that death may have stopped being pornographic. In the past, television and the other media spoke only euphemistically about death. Today dying, grieving, loss and bereavement are becoming parts of our reality. Palliative care promotes a hope that lives through death. Stoddard (1992) observes that the quaint phrase that someone has "lost" a husband, wife or baby is ironic. But we do not lose loved ones. Love does not know time; love is always present perfect tense (p. 223). The inclusion of families in terminal treatment infuses the cycle of birth and transcends generations with the passage of dying. The whole person, the continuity of self and identity are celebrated and made possible by human connections that transcend death. The hospice is more than buildings and treatment centers. It gives a new meaning to the concept of continuity of care, between people and across generations.

Home Health Care

Another program area that can help older adults enjoy their lives to the fullest, even in the face of physical limitations or illness, is a well-conceived home health care and community services program. If one were to devise a user unfriendly health care system for older adults, it would be a system that forces the patient to come to the treating professional instead of the treatment coming to the patient. Traditional health care systems (particularly in the United States) have been reluctant to return to the tradition of house calls. In Great Britain, home health services are available to older adults through their national system. A well-conceived and ethically planned home health care system provides a variety of services that are available to seniors in their community or home.

In the United States since 1996 there has been a tragic series of reported fraud and abuse in home health care widely reported in national news. While this problem must be addressed and reversed it could be even more tragic if home services to elders are removed. Making health care accesible for patients and not just convenient for professionals is pivotal in humane treatment. The quest for good models and places of enlightened, committed and concerned treatment are more crucial than ever.

One example of excellent home health care is a visiting nurses' association that has combined with the county social services organization in New Hampshire. When last cited, this nursing program was based out of Keene, Charlestown, Wilton and Peterborough, New Hampshire. This home health care and community organization project includes private duty nursing programs for specialized patient needs, consultation and service through a hospice program, an adult group day care program, a child health care program, a prenatal care program and available industrial nursing care as well. This integrated system is "just what the Doctor ordered," if the doctor did not have to worry about whether her programs fit into the existing health care system. These kinds of programs provide strong and focused services, particularly in the area of rehabilitation and prevention with a focus on continuity of care. Acute care has been the purview of hospitals. Support for model innovative home health programs like these in New Hampshire can guarantee that prevention and recovery need not be the forgotten dimensions of health care. In addition, home health care increasingly offers acute in-home services such as IVs, chemotherapy, multiple lab tests and insulin therapy adjustments. Continuity of care can exist. Another quality of this program is that it has been nestled in a deep appreciation of the traditions and culture of New England. Services are offered from cradle to grave, from prenatal programs to hospice. Administrators (notably Virginia S. Vidaver, executive director) of home care programs tell us that development and preservation of such programs represent a constant political struggle. They must be cost effective within the larger framework of a pressured health care system; they must seek external funding such as programs through the United Way in the United States, and they must also strive to make their programs reimbursable under existing federal programs such as Medicare. Preserving easy access programs such as these means that administrators must be skilled and focused in services but also wizards in the politics of changing health care systems.

Another hopeful trend in home health care is the creation of a small but growing Academy of Home Care Physicians. Retsinas (p. 139, 1995) cited a recent American Medical Association survey which showed that of 1,100 primary care physicians sampled, half made home visits. Furthermore, new home care technologies described as "home telemedicine" may soon allow video visits to a patient home via video telephone boxes. This technology will supplement periodic visits in person by physician or nurse. The Retsinas article entitled, "Back to the Future—Housecalls," suggests that creative use of new technology could augment traditional house calls, creating more accessible medical care with the human touch.

Memory Clinics

What problem affects about twenty percent of all individuals over 65 and more than fifty percent of those over 85? What problem causes fear, worry and even depression in many seniors? Most physicians would include arthritis, coronary artery disease, cataract and various cancers without a mention of memory problems. The attitude of many primary physicians has been to dismiss memory complaints automatically or not aggressively pursue their etiology when other medical problems need addressed.

The State of Florida has created a unique program to target the escalating problem of progressive dementias by funding a number of specialized and accessible clinics through its Alzheimer's Disease Initiative. The East Central Florida Memory Disorder Clinic (MDC), one of eight clinics funded by the state, brings a unique perspective that allows participation of the entire community of seniors and their families. At this clinic, free memory screening and evaluation services are integrated and coordinated with comprehensive follow-up programs involving the medical, psychological and family aspects of these problems. The majority of people screened do not have true dementing disease, so the user—friendly climate of the clinic makes it safe for patients and their families to discover other causes for memory problems such as depression, stress, reactions to medication or to the medical conditions or benign but common worries. The sevices of the clinic include a good clinical and psychological history, a well—designed brief neuropsychological screening, a caring triage to help patients navigate the puzzling health system, involvement in a state and national research consortium (Consortium to Establish a Registry for Alzheimers Disease or CERAD) with multiagency affilitation plus a wide range of caregiver education and support groups and preventive programs.

Approved by the state legislature in 1990, the MDC was an initiative of Holmes Regional Hospital and Florida Institute of Technology with assistance from Melbourne Neurologic Clinic and the local Easter Seals Society. The MDC serves the community by providing the array of services described above. In addition, clinical psychology doctoral students at Florida Tech's School of Psychology are integrated in the service, education and research dimensions of the clinic. Their clinical services are learned and delivered in a way that trains them to honor the unique resource seniors represent while providing informed and caring treatment with an appreciation of the medical, psychological and spiritual dimensions of healthy aging. The clinic also provides educational programs for the general public, professional caregivers and community organizations. Using a model of active assertive outreach and continuity of care, the clinic benefits patients and their families while raising the consciousness of the lay and professional community about healthy aging and the problems of dementing diseases. The doctoral students involved also tell us it's fun.

Ecumenical Pastoral Counseling Services

The value and viability of an ecumenical pastoral counseling service presents a healthy model of helping people age well psychologically, spiritually and even physically. An excellent example of such a center exists in the Tidewater area of southeastern Virginia; the Tidewater Pastoral Counseling Service. This center has developed a model that answers many of the questions and dilemmas about how to provide the best services and create funding alternatives to the medical health system model.

This particular agency, Tidewater Pastoral Counseling Services (TPCS), is in its twentieth year of providing services to the community and region it serves. The Center has joined with the community in order to provide prevention and treatment not only for individuals but also families, churches and synagogues. The Center began working out of the extra offices of The First Presbyterian church in Norfolk, Virginia in the late 1970's. The original founders (including the current director, Reverend William Hedrick) sought to provide counseling services to that church and its community. Given the good response, the original staff expanded to include clergy from a variety of Protestant, Catholic and Jewish orientations. This development occurred by attempting to duplicate the quality of services offered at the first church. Then they expanded the model to other church and temple communities in this sprawling metropolitan area of over 1,500,000 people in seven cities. The clergy who serve TPCS are drawn from a variety of backgrounds. At various times, there have been Catholic nuns, lay clergy, ordained clergy from most Protestant religions and rabbis and counselors serving the Jewish community. Many of the counselors have been retired military chaplains, and at times, retired physicians have also consulted to the agency. The credentials of these therapists are strong within their own pastoral counseling professions, and many of the staff hold clinical or diplomate status in the American Association for Pastoral Counseling. Many are licensed in another mental health field in addition to or instead of their primary pastoral identity.

One of the unique accomplishments of the Center is its creation of a network of satellites that are housed in various parishes or religious communities in the area. The staff may serve as "circuit riders" who go to the home temple or church one or two days a week. The local congregation supports the idea of having well—trained counselors or psychotherapists who are also spiritually attuned to the values of parishioners. Arrangements have usually been made whereby the local congregation contributes money to help subsidize the cost of counseling. The staff of the pastoral counseling service is also able to use office space with minimal cost. The counseling service provides psychoeducational, wellness and health-focused workshops for the temple or parish community in addition to the counseling services.

Another valuable component of the Center is its educational programs for clergy and other mental health professionals and physicians in the area. For instance, TPCS offers training workshops to parish ministers on facets of counseling with individual problems or for family and couples issues. The training is devised so that clergy can further their own credentials and knowledge in psychotherapy, counseling and preventive mental health. The Center has even developed affiliation with universities whereby pastoral counselors in the Tidewater area can earn advanced degrees. The interchange through this educational effort not only ensures that the staff of the center is well educated and energized by interaction, but also that the community is educated about treatment and prevention, as well as the psychological, physical and spiritual dimensions of health and healing.

The Center also has helped sponsor and support a program called the Ghent Venture. Ghent is the community in which the original church is located. TPCS works with the community and population of Ghent to create a forum for workshops, education, art and community interaction focused particularly on the senior community.

In summary, the Tidewater Pastoral Counseling Service has developed a way of providing continuity of care. It offers acute treatment, prevention and educational services to individuals, families, congregations and communities in a creative format. It has also devised a creative way to develop funding and support for services that are largely outside the medical health care system. By developing alternative funding, it has also strengthened the relationship between church and temple communities and has provided for excellent psychological services with an informed spiritual dimension.

Elderhostel

Elderhostel is more a movement than a place; it is actually many wonderful places and encompasses many vital seniors.

At the leading edge of the older population is a core of people who are young-old, affluent-old, and educated-old, an assertive middle class constituency that is increasingly conscious of the options still available to them. These are the elders who are ready—physically, mentally, and financially—for new experiences. The number of healthy elders with ample financial resources has created a vast market for programs that satisfy the need for self-fulfillment. As we have moved beyond a deficient medical model for aging to one that stresses opportunities, rather than limits, millions of elders have rejected roles of disengagement and have opened themselves to new ideas. (Mills, 1993, p. 150)

Since 1975 when Elderhostel began at the University of New Hampshire, the program has grown from an enrollment of 220 to a worldwide program with over 234,000 participants annually in fifty countries. More than half a million people receive the Elderhostel catalogs that describe course offerings and travel arrangements. The locations and course topics boggle the mind, with committed and fascinating presenters in locations that vary from quaint, historic, and picturesque to elegant and inspiring. The programs and travels are affordable, and offered by teachers who love their topics and their homeland. The director of a local program told Rosalyn and Jimmy Carter (prominent supporters of Elderhostel) that her goal for each program is to take the large, diverse group of people previously unknown to each other and provide them with an educational and social experience that they will never forget.

Elderhostel's original spirit or intent to preserve each country or locale's unique flavor has been preserved in their course offerings. A founder, Marty Knowlton, would not allow his brainchild to become "the MacDonald's of older adult education." Each Elderhostel program is unique and distinct, preserving the character and philosophy of the host institution. Each campus thinks of the program as truly its own. Elderhostel combines the excitement and challenge of travel with the enrichment of courses on interesting topics, taught by highly qualified teachers in surroundings they love. One- two- or three-week programs bring together groups of 15 to 40 people over the age of 60 at college campuses, conference centers or retreats. Students delve into the subject matter for the sheer joy of learning. Elderhostel embodies a vitality, creativity, growth and relatedness that is the envy of people at any age.

The interested reader can contact Elderhostel at 75 Federal Street, Boston, Massachusetts, 02110. Their phone is (617) 426-5437.

Cross-Generational Communities

At a conference of medical, psychological and religious leaders which the author attended in Virginia in 1993, the topic was aging and the three dimensions of health. The participants frequently talked about the importance of interaction between older adults, with the generation before them, and perhaps even more importantly with those who would be the age of their grandchildren. There are predictable stages in an individual's lifelong development. We also know that there are predictable stages in a family life cycle. Both psychological help and tension come from the collision of individual and family life stage needs. That is one of the main reasons why interaction between the generations is the best way to know problems and solutions across the generations. A powerful harmony can develop as grandparents, children and grandchildren interact freely. This interaction need not be limited to family members. Much benefit comes from caring elders interacting with people the age of their children and grandchildren in a cross-generational setting.

This idea of a generational interaction was warmly supported by the participants in the conference. Interestingly, the medical and psychological professionals began to speculate how such a community could be developed. There was great enthusiasm and discussion about ways to fund, to create a valuable mix and to ensure a shared ethic in such a community. The well—meaning but nearsighted medical and psychological professionals missed the point, causing a spiritual leader to ask, "Have you ever heard of temples or churches?" We overlooked the cross-generational resource churches can provide. There is a fine tradition of religious community centers across the country, rich in cross-generational problems and solutions. Churches, temples and religious centers represent established and vital incubators for cross-generational living, loving and learning. Keeping such centers psychologically and physically healthy makes them even better.

No Ageism—Shared History (Cohorts) and Shared Cultures

When meeting, understanding and working with seniors (or any age), knowledge of their most vivid or influential shared history becomes a powerful ally. This shared critical history has to do with the major events of a country, region, community, culture or society. For example World War I and its aftermath, the stock market crash of 1929 and the ensuing depression, Prohibition and its repeal, the New Deal, World War II and its aftermath, McCarthyism, the civil rights movement, Sputnik and the Cold War, Vietnam and its repurcussions, and currently the computer technology/information age are all examples of the shared history of different generations. The research in aging quite unpoetically calls these *age cohort* experiences.

In a slightly more entertaining way a psychologist, J. R. Sehulster (1996), showed how people's identities are shaped by pivotal memories that coincide with *shared eras*. In a study asking people to list motion pictures that defined their era, Sehulster found that movies (or other influences like music, theater, books or "first experiences") seen between the ages of 14 and 24 seemed to capture the person's sense of "my era." Understanding these historic landscapes or influential eras improves our ability to know and help others. That knowledge gives valuable insight into people's challenges, losses, hopes and strengths in facing adversity.

Recalling the quote at the start of this chapter "life is what happens to you when you're planning something else," we find that these historical events and eras define some of life's big surprises. They help define our character and they change our individual and collective life stories. They are a shared stage or backdrop in which each individual or family's story is intertwined. Knowing the challenges and themes of a generation's shared story can make people more comfortable in exploring their individual and family stories. Appreciating these shared histories helps those with whom we work view us as health professionals who are aware and concerned.

Another part of a healthy model is a place without ageism. A psychiatrist, Allan Chinen (1989), has compiled a fascinating book, telling fairy tales about seniors from different cultures. His creative anthology can increase our appreciation of a mature life. In the United States we are not noted for honoring older adults. Chinen draws from a variety of cultures and countries in which traditional fairy tales give respect, focus, purpose and health to the second half of life. The stories are full of irony, but are also deeply appreciative of the struggles and joys of growing older. Some of these wise tales are described further in Chapter four. Every effort to recognize and combat ageism helps create healthy places for healthy aging.

HUMOR AND ADAPTATION, IRONY AND LAUGHTER

Any healthy model also includes a sense of humor. If a culture, guild or institution takes itself too seriously, its healthy value can be diminished. If the task of aging is approached in too serious a fashion, the journey of life may not be much better than a forced march. The ability to balance change with continuity is helped greatly by a sense of irony and humor. So much of life, particularly the second half of life, involves an acceptance that we cannot change everything. We may save our energy by not swimming against currents that needlessly exhaust and frustrate us. Without a doubt, the healthiest seniors with whom we have worked have provided an anthology of energizing jokes and inspiring aphorisms. The following quotes are a healthy reminder that life should not be all work and ordeal. Laughter and irony help the process of adaptation and renewal.

> There is no problem so great it can't be solved by a long walk.
> > —S. Kierkegaard

> Some things are too important to be taken seriously.
> > —Oscar Wilde

> You don't stop laughing because you grow old; you grow old because you stop laughing.
> > —Michael Pritchard

> If you live long enough, you are revered; rather like an old building.
> > —Ambrose Bierce

> When a thing has been said and said well, have no scruple. Take it and copy it.
> > —Anatole France

> Reality is a collective hunch.
> > —Lily Tomlin and Jane Wagner

> It is okay to laugh in the bedroom so long as you don't point.
> > —Will Durst

Irony can lead to a sense of perspective; what is good, what is lasting, when to push, when to coast and when to change direction. That gift of perspective is what Erikson's (1982) last four life stages (identity, intimacy, generativity and integrity) can offer in abundance.

4

Healthy Stories and Aging Well

This chapter is about preventing, living through and growing from change, difficulty and illness. A theme running throughout the book is that keeping a healthy identity in the face of expected and unexpected challenges throughout life is a task of story telling and story tending. People live as individuals, as friends and lovers, as family and as part of cultures. We have learned that healthy stories are about physical, psychological and spiritual beings. We would like to suggest some important principles and valuable stories that help us remember who we are, shape who we are becoming and foster a sense of perspective and humor throughout life.

Erik Erikson's (1982) cycle of eight life eras is universally taught to health professionals but rarely fully understood. The last four stages identity, intimacy, generativity and integrity (adolescence, early and middle adulthood, through the oldest old), reveal crucial and profound secrets. The real-life dilemmas and solutions in those life phases translate theory into humanity. If the challenges are fully recognized, we may be able to honor and foster healthy life stories when we hear one.

What follows is a consideration of principles for healthy stories or life narratives. The healthy stories are about individuals, friendships, families and communities. We will sketch some principles for healthy stories in each of these facets of our lives. We will share a few quotes to set the tone and will clarify some things we have learned from counseling older adults in a variety of settings.   The headings are prompted by Erikson's (1982) four stages of the second half of life.

IDENTITY (FIDELITY)

Individual Stories

> When I was younger I could remember everything, whether it happened or not.
> —Mark Twain

> The mask, given time comes to be the face itself.
> —Marguerite Yourcenar

> I'd enjoy talking with you but I feel a bit guilty and hypocritical. Between the things I've forgotten, the things I've repressed and the things I will not discuss, there's not much left.
> —91 year old women (interviewed for the book *The Ageless Self*)

In her book, *The Ageless Self*, Sharon Kaufman (1986) tells us that agelessness is a matter of people being able to find meaning in life by "telling their life story." That is not to say that the telling or the living of one's life story is an easy-flowing narrative. Rather, Kaufman found that by listening with respect and empathy to the many older adults she studied, she heard stories that made sense of what was valuable, difficult and meaningful in their lives. This adventure was built on stories about their lives. Individuals could recount themes at different phases in their lives. Kaufman discovered that they did not think of the meaning in their lives as anchored to stages or ages. Rather, the identity flowed through themes. Those people who seemed most integrated or healthier were able to make sense of some of the senselessness in their lives by clarifying the meaning of important experiences. A person thereby puts mistakes, tragedies or windfalls into an understandable focus.

> You need only claim the events of your life to make yourself yours.
> —Florida Scott-Maxwell (age 80)

> The old are unsure of a future, their past is growing stale
> so they are dependent on the sentience of the moment. It
> behooves us to be sentient. The old by recalling the
> past, are fascinated by the query of what future is possi-
> ble. Their present is empty. *Or* — there is nothing of in-
> terest to be said about the old, except that they are ab-
> sorbed by age. Each could be true. One takes one's
> choice.
> —Florida Scott-Maxwell (age 82) *The*
> *Measure of My Days*

In the same vein as Kaufman's (1986) notions about the importance of narrative or life stories, George Howard (1991) also views
self-understanding as a process of telling a story and elaborating that
story about one's life. Howard suggests that the development of an
identity is an issue of life story construction; that psychopathology is a
matter of one's life story gone awry; and that psychotherapy can be an
exercise in story repair.

> Time is not line but a dimension. You don't look back
> along time but down through it, like water. Sometimes
> this comes to the surface, sometimes that, sometimes
> nothing. Nothing goes away.
> —Margaret Atwood, *Cat's Eye*

The healthy stories of individuals are marked by a sense of
identity and fidelity, preserved (even though modified at different life
stages) throughout the lifespan. Providing an ear to listen to those stories encourages a work in progress, an honoring and an enduring meaning to those lives.

INTIMACY (LOVE)

Friendship, Love and Intimate Stories

Eidetic People
Life stories are about friends as well as about ourselves.
Enemies, lovers and heroes are also important relationships in our life

stories. Our memories and our stories remind us of who we have been and who we are in relation to these important people. Harry Stack Sullivan, the noted psychiatrist, suggested that we all have what he called *eidetic people* who have influenced our lives. Eidetic people are those flesh and blood, vivid personalities who affect us by their memory. Consider for a moment the people who have shaped your own life most. With a little prodding and not much effort, we can quickly call back these human stories. Eidetic people include that third grade teacher who shaped you into believing in yourself. An eidetic person could be the friend who supported you by listening to you mourn and talk about the experience of another's death. An eidetic person is the mentor who inspired you to follow a life path. An eidetic person could be the one who taught you that a sense of humor mixes liberally with a sense of importance.

In counseling combat veterans over the years, we learned that they often have traumatic vivid recollections. These haunting flashbacks are sometimes called flash-bulb memories. On a positive note, important people in our lives may be just as vivid a memory but can project a positive influence. Eidetic people are ingrained images who shape us in ways we only partially realize. Friends, family, enemies and lovers can support us or consume us, but they always affect us. These eidetic people endure longer than the flashbulb effect. We carry their image and influence as a private legacy.

A supervisor of the author disclosed a secret in counseling couples. The supervisor was asked, how can you tell if a couple will make it through a crisis? How can you tell if the fights and arguments outweigh the benefits of continuing the relationship? How can you tell if the commitment can be repaired? This supervisor said that it is rare for a couple to stay together if they no longer like the smell and taste of each other. That may not always be true, but it certainly is a vivid image and recollection.

A psychiatrist, Frank Pittman (1989), has described the variations of infidelity. His book *Private Lies* describes the variants on affairs, philandering, deceit and divorce. His readable reflections lead to important principles and qualities that promote lasting fidelity in romantic relationships. Among the crucial principles Pittman suggests are the following: fidelity is a decision, honesty is central in intimacy and marital conflict should help clarify the issues and emotions (rather than determine a winner or loser) (Pittman, 1989, pp. 275–285). The concept of good faith or commitment to the marriage can help change and strengthen the relationship now and give the couple a strategy to use for future growth and intimacy.

While counseling older couples we have heard amazing stories about the twists and turns, about the teases and tortures, and about the power of memories and love. These stories are amazing, horrifying and inspiring. If we listen well and provide a safe place for them to remember (out loud), the listening lets them recall, reclaim or discover their own wisdom. Stories of these relationships and their twists and turns can be used to play back old solutions that help them with current dilemmas. This reservoir of memories can help us make sense of our current lives by drawing on old memories and friends. These influences can comfort us when those eidetic people are far away or even after they have died. The number of widowed people who continue to converse with their deceased spouse is frequent and at times valuable. This way of coping bears out the importance of these memorable influences.

Friendly Stories

Some principles accompany healthy relationships. These qualities touch on issues of commitment, understanding, passion, inspiration, anger and enduring caring. They are about wounds and healing. There is even a creativity that allows friendship or a marriage to be reformed and renewed in response to challenges and opportunities at different life stages. Let us look into some of these healthy principles based on healthy stories we have heard.

In social psychology research on friendships, there is an important principle about self-concept and close friends. We share our personal stories with our closest friends. For the most part, our closest friends are people who share our view of ourselves. It is a kind of mutual validation. It is a way of supporting, challenging and treasuring our friends and confirming our stories about each other and ourselves. Through day-to-day interactions we share disappointments and surprise, and we attempt to make meaning of current happenings. Our life stories are shaped with and by our friends in this daily narrative. A friendship is a safe place to try out our understanding, our bets on what is important. In this way friendships help verify the unfolding story of our lives.

An interesting irony, however, is that when a large discrepancy exists between our view of ourselves and our friend's view of us, this uncomfortable rift can actually lead to a distancing, if not an ending to a friendship. We seek out affirmation from friends to validate the way we see ourselves. The converse is probably true. That is, enemies, or people with whom we are angry, view us as opposite of the way we see ourselves. The stories we tell! This principle is important in understanding the value of psychotherapy. When there is a discrepancy between our view of ourselves and the way a friend views us, the friendship may end unless a new description or changed self-story is adopted (or the friend changes their view to agree with us). In contrast, therapy serves to clarify, validate, yet critique a person's life story. The value of therapy may begin at a place where friendships end. By this we mean that psychotherapy is uniquely suited to continue a relationship past the point of challenging a person's story about themselves. This transition, beyond just validating another, is a way to preserve our best qualities and modify our worst ones. This balance can help shape our past, our present and our emergence by rewriting the story. Our closest friends share our view of us. The more enduring friendships are ones that can last through different versions of stories about ourselves and about our friendships. Friends support us, define us and challenge us, and the best ones care for us by forgiving old and inspiring new stories.

The interpersonal dimension, of healthy stories and aging well is marked by Erikson's (1982) themes of intimacy versus isolation. These friendly stories are about sharing and vulnerability, and a balance of independence and dependence.

Another theme that runs through stories we have heard about friends and spouses is a paradox: the principle sometimes called *reversal*. This subtle law of attraction shows that the qualities that initially attract us to someone often become the qualities that irritate us most later in the relationship. For instance, we often see couples deeply embroiled in conflict. A common example is that one person views the other as too irresponsible, too unpredictable or too flippant. That "culprit" views the "accuser" as too rigid, too serious and even too stifling. The funny part is that when asked what attracted them to each other in the first place, the "culprit" usually liked the reliability, the stability and the clear vision of the "accuser." Conversely, the "accuser" was attracted to the spontaneity, unpredictability and adventurous nature of the partner at the beginning of the relationship.

Jungian psychology has suggested that we unconsciously expect that by merging with another, we can incorporate his or her admirable qualities. Unfortunately, merger does not guarantee that we annex another's qualities simply by loving them. The quality of attraction becomes the source of irritation; that is the reversal. In a way, that irritating quality reminds us of an undeveloped dimension in our own personality. If we only blame the other person, that projected anger can interfere with our own development. All sorts of other examples and variations on this theme of attraction, irritation and possible personality growth could be retold.

A compelling paradox in intimate relations involves control and vulnerability. This story has the following plot. Most people seek a satisfying relationship or enduring intimacy. In seeking such an important relationship, people have contradictory needs. On the one hand, if a relationship is to be healthy, each person must exert a certain amount of control or influence. If there is not enough control, the person could reduce or lose his or her own sense of self. In a healthy relationship, we need to be able to express our own needs in a direct fashion to meet mutual needs. However, sometimes in desperation people seek so much control or influence in the relationship that the control actually thwarts intimacy. The second part of the paradox is a need to be vulnerable. The relationship must be safe enough to be vulnerable. Closeness and intimacy emerge from vulnerability, from owning our softest qualities in a place of safety. Some people believe or have a hunch that if they are vulnerable and deferring in a relationship, they will be loved. They could give away their identity without a balance of influence or leverage. The paradox, then, is that we must be careful of what we wish for. Intimacy and satisfying relationships are a balance of control and vulnerability. If we gain too much control in a relationship, pursuing our hunch, we may find that we have sacrificed vulnerability and no one can get close to us. The converse is true. If out of love and caring we are completely deferring and vulnerable in a relationship, we may not exert sufficient leverage to ensure that intimacy in this relationship can last. A shared commitment to a relationship and a realization that control and vulnerability must be balanced are the secret ingredients for a resilient and enduring intimacy.

In clinical practice, the people on the "control" end of the relationship spectrum tend to show symptoms of stress-related problems stemming from their belief that they must not be vulnerable. These symptoms include stomach disorders, high blood pressure, stress headaches and the like. People who believe that being vulnerable will produce intimacy tend to show symptoms such as depression, anxiety and a martyred interpersonal style.

Intimacy comes from being able to define a relationship so that each person has a balance of influence alongside vulnerability. Shared control and shared vulnerability can breathe love and vitality into the relationship.

Rebalancing or redefining an intimate relationship has been called "rewriting love stories," by Hudson and O'Hanlon (1991). These marital therapists describe approaches that reframe old dilemmas, remove blame and change bad strategies for resolving conflict. They do it with humor and narrative. They describe how humor helps by "degrimming" a couple's loss or tragedy. They use a technique that they call the "Martian's guide to intimacy" as a funny way to put couples at ease, to force a new perspective and to rewrite love stories. This approach gives license to start all over without old assumptions or expectations.

The ability to redefine a relationship, to create a new story about a relationship throughout the lifespan, is a secret of enduring friendship and intimacy. If that fact is not understood, a series of broken relationships, marriages and friendships may appear as a pattern in one's life. The notion of preserving an identity in the face of life's unexpected challenges is true of loves and friendships as well as individual life stories. A quote already used in Chapter two is worth repeating.

> Everything that irritates about others can lead us to an understanding of ourselves.
> —C. G. Jung

Some other useful quotes on this topic include the following:

> One does not make friends. One recognizes them.
> —Garth Henricks

> If two people agree on everything, one of them is unnecessary.
> —George Bernard Shaw

A friend is one who knows all about you and loves you
just the same.
        —Elbert Hubbard

He had no faults God pays any attention to.
                —From a Eulogy for Art Rooney, Owner of
                the Pittsburgh Steelers

Animal Friends

A wonderful discovery for healthy stories with older adults is
the importance of animals. Any family knows the value of a pet.
There is a growing formal recognition of the importance of animals
through an organization called the Delta Society, a nonprofit organization founded in 1977. The aims of the Delta Society are to improve
human health and well-being "by promoting mutually beneficial con-
tacts," among people, animals and nature. Some of the work by psychologist James Lynch (1979) in Philadelphia has shown that the availability of a pet and a relationship with an animal mitigated against heart
disease. Beyond any focused benefit to prevent illness, pets are a lively,
emotionally connected and enduring source of love and relatedness.
Enjoy the following few quotes and refer to the Reference section for information on the benefits of animals in prevention, treatment, and rehabilitation. (Anderson, 1975; Corson and Corson, 1982; Fogle, 1981;
Friedman, Katacher, Lynch and Thomas, 1980; Katacher, 1982; Lynch,
1979; Muschel, 1984; Ptak, 1995; Robb, Boyd and Pritash, 1980;
Siegel, 1990; Thomas, 1993).

The great pleasure of a dog is that you may make a fool of
yourself with him and not only will he not scold you, but
he will make a fool of himself too.
        —Samuel Butler

Animals are such agreeable friends—they ask no questions, they pass no criticisms.
        —George Eliot

Heaven goes by favor; if it went by merit, you would stay
out and your dog would go in.
        —Mark Twain

The reader interested in animal friends can support and pursue the movement through a national society in the United States. They can be contacted at this address:

> The Delta Society
> P.O. Box 1080
> Renton, WA 98057–9906
> (206) 266-7357 or
> NY (212) 310-2802

GENERATIVITY (CARE)

Family Stories and Legacies

As noted earlier, it is said that families should give us "roots and wings." Psychology's fancy name for this is *individuation*. Individuation is a unique balance of autonomy and relatedness. Our ability to be close and yet maintain our own identity is a gift influenced by the family in which we grew up. These are important things to learn from our family and to teach to our children. This ability can sometimes be good news and sometimes bad news because the ways we love and relate are learned and taught automatically. Healthy ways of loving (without smothering) and encouraging (without abandoning) can forecast how well we will enjoy our aging years (Kerr and Bowen, 1988).

The following quotes scatter different thoughts on the theme of healthy family stories.

> There are only two or three human stories, and they go on repeating themselves as fiercely as if they had never happened before.
> —Willa Cather

> Happiness is having a large, loving, caring, close-knit family in another city.
> —George Burns

> Have children while your parents are still young enough to take care of them.
> —Rita Rudner

It is also fascinating to have people think back through their family tree, their genogram. To listen to these stories is to recount wonderful legacies, frightening tragedies, and threads of a family's identity throughout the generations (Roberto, 1992). The following Pakistani folk tale is an ironic and interesting example.

> An ancient grandmother lived with her daughter and grandson. As she grew frail and feeble, instead of being a help around the house, she became a constant trial. She broke plates and cups, lost knives and spilled water. The daughter sent the grandson to buy his grandmother a wooden plate. The boy hesitated because he knew a wooden plate would humiliate his grandmother. But his mother insisted, so off he went. He returned bringing not one, but two wooden plates. "I only asked you to buy one," his mother said. "Didn't you hear me?" "Yes," said the boy. "But I bought the second one so there would be one for you when you get old."
> —Pakistani folktale

As we have listened to people talk about their families, we have been impressed by the importance of family rituals. In some families, these rituals are truly rigid and are preserved religiously. When families get together around holidays and birthdays, for instance, their rituals preserve connection and honor. Sometimes these gatherings are the backdrop for chaos. That is to say that rituals are no guarantee that the family's ways of relating will go smoothly. However, the value and preservation of rituals can span times of conflict and keep the connection throughout the years. Often a family starting a new generation will create their own rituals (or even an antiritual to one that irritated them in the family in which they grew up). We do find, however, that many healthy people not only have evolved rituals for their family, but have also made a strong commitment to these rituals as a means to generativity and emotional health.

Family stories are generational legacies, not just one person's life story. These stories and legacies sometimes heal and sometimes curse us. Their power for healthy aging is strongest when we know how the tributaries flow across our ancestry.

A book by Robert Akeret (1991) explains ways to gather the stories of a lifetime and share them with one's family. Not only does this well-described process validate a personal identity, but it also creates a healing cross-generational way to build bridges and span understanding. This family force is a source of energy, meaning and love.

> When a knowledgeable old person dies, a whole library disappears.
> —African proverb

Sandy, an African American friend of the senior author, invited him to her wedding. She observed that in slave days, blacks were prohibited from practicing rituals since they promoted a sense of connection and family identity. She said that at her wedding the bride and groom would jump over a broom together, since this tradition was one of the rare rituals preserved (smuggled), and practiced during the era of slavery. The ritual reminds us of oppression and emerging freedom through a love that lasts across generations.

INTEGRITY (WISDOM)

Life Review and the End Game

Erikson's (1982) discovery and description of the last developmental stage (Integrity vs. Despair) hopefully leads to a satisfied, yet realistic, wisdom. The stories at this life juncture may be the most inspiring or the most anguished. This stage is a harvesting of life's loves and labors. Sometimes this stage is hastened in people's lives by existential jolts like catastrophic illness or the loss of people or places we love. Healthy stories in this phase build on the generativity of prior life stages. As a life is reviewed and reconsidered from the end perspective, there is an enduring meaning. What was important and lasting? What was hollow or misguided? How do you close? How do you end?

A popular idiom in America these days is the phrase *the end game*. The end game conjures images of urgently dissolving a sport or gamble. How do people deal with this finale? How do they tell the last episode? Do they panic? Do they continue new verses of the same life lyric? Do they, "burn and rave at close of day," and "rage against the dying of the light," while they, "do not go gentle into that good night?" (Dylan Thomas, 1946, p. 128).   Can they still appreciate irony? A clergy friend said he noticed that people in their twilight years often begin serious reading of their Bible. Although he knew he should be gratified by this trend, the clergy also humorously called it, "studying for your final exam." Cramming for finals often is not enough without prior preparation. Nevertheless, the end story is an opportunity to put things in perspective and pass along the joys, dangers and secrets of the journey.

> Wisdom is the art of knowing what to overlook.
> —William James

Cultural Stories

Cultural stories talk about ethnic backgrounds, a little about political movements, and wonderful rituals, legends and passions. Our social contexts, our work contexts and our social meanings are an important backdrop for a person's life story.

Culture, community and family stories can give us meaningful answers to the questions about what endures, the legacies that span generations. Erik Erikson's concept of generativity is a matter of legacy. Some legacies are far sighted, guiding and inspiring; unfortunately, some people's legacies are oppressive, conflicted and uncertain. Fairy tales and culture tales are examples of what Jung called the collective unconscious (Campbell, 1988).

> A folk fairy tale . . . is the result of a story being shaped and reshaped by being told millions of times, by different adults to all kinds of other adults and children. Each narrator, as he told the story, dropped and added elements to make it more meaningful to himself and to the listeners whom he knew well.
> —Bruno Bettelheim, *The Uses of Enchantment*

> Deeper meaning resides in the fairy tales told to me in my childhood than in the truth that is taught by life.
> —Schiller, *The Piccolomini III*

Child of pure unclouded brow and dreaming eyes of wonder! Tho times be fleet, and I and thou are half a life asun-
der, thy loving smile will surely hail the love-gift of a
fairy tale.
> —C. L. Dodgson (Lewis Carroll), *Through the
> Looking Glass*

Alan Chinen (1989) describes seven vital tasks that confront a
person from midlife on. These themes are common to elder tales or the
cultural stories that have evolved across recorded history. Chinen's
book is a fascinating compilation of fairy tales drawn from a number of
countries and traditions. The fairy tales he has chosen convey a value
and wisdom born of successful aging and valuing older adults in different cultures. Among the traditions and countries sampled are the
Jewish tradition, Japan, Asia Minor, Croatia, Italy, Arabia, India,
Germany, Korea and Burma.

The first task deals with multiple losses and fear of decline.
The older person finds that age and experience may provide new
strengths to fight old fears. The challenge of maturity is to grow
through these setbacks. A second challenge involves self-confrontation
and self-reformation. Especially in myth and fairy tales, Jung's influences are recurrent. Learning to make peace with one's darker side or
the qualities that we try to hide can be a process of growth and improvement. Chinen feels that a third challenge is the need to develop an
empathic understanding of human nature. From this understanding,
worldly wisdom can grow. Through the advantage of years of experience, older adults can create wise perspectives, based on psychological
insights. These insights translate into a personal wisdom that benefits
others when shared. By letting go of overvalued objects, or the accu-
mulation of possessions, as well as short-sighted youthful preoccupa-
tions, a reverence and empathy for life can emerge. The wisdom also
helps us avoid unnecessary adversaries and lets us pace ourselves for the
stresses and challenges of the second half of life.

A fourth challenge is the value of self-transcendence. This
transcendence comes from letting go or discarding dreams and personal
ambitions that may have obsessed us at earlier times. The possibility
of turning to more noble endeavors, like Erikson's task of generativity,
can do two things. The self transcendence can extend the value of our
efforts while also providing a source of energy and power beyond our-

selves. Chinen feels that the mature adult returns to the transcendent inspirations of his or her youth reclaiming the idealistic motivations of younger years. The return to these earlier inspiring values reflects a deeper understanding which allows us to bring some of the dreams to fruition.

A fifth challenge is described as emancipated innocence. This is actually regaining the spontaneity we knew in childhood. Youth's innocence and naive creativity can be integrated with adult wisdom and mature judgment. This process is most likely to occur if the individual succeeds at the self-confrontation and self-transcendence described earlier. Again, this positive outcome is what Erikson called a self-integrity or a sense of self-affirmation. Stagnation and despair may be the result if these tasks are not navigated.

The reclaiming of wonder and delight in life is Chinen's sixth challenge. The world is no longer taken for granted if every new instance is appreciated. Both Carl Jung and Abraham Maslow linked enlightenment to healthy maturation. That is not to say that enlightenment is a common occurrence in the second half of life. It is, however, a useful aspiration. Chinen feels that the achievement of some enlightenment is what distinguishes the elder from the elderly; hence, the function of the elder tales is to appreciate the highest measure of humanity. This creates an ideal to strive toward rather than an average to settle for (Chinen, 1989).

The seventh challenge is to provide both practical counsel and noble inspiration to the young. If older adults are valued, they will be sought out as mentors, creating a rare rapprochement between secular society and transcendent truth. Culture tales or fairy tales that value older adults are the opposite of ageism. Valuing elders' wisdom teaches us what can be, in spite of human limitations. This way of caring and learning honors the next generation as well as the elder.

> Advocacy is often expressed through spirituality and elders are among the most vigilant workers in religious groups.
> —Dan Blazer, M.D., Duke University

One caveat probably should be registered. The benefit of focusing on the highest possibilities, achievements or wisdoms of older adults cannot be overemphasized. The caution, however, is that we should not romanticize old age so much that despair results if people fall short of the ideal. A pressure to be wise, resourceful, energetic and inspiring is a heavy burden. We simply hope that the aspirations do not become an unnecessary pressure to measure one's self against a rare standard. An inspiring balance (between stories of what can be and what may not be) is the beacon that lights a path of generativity for the children who follow.

REVISING STORIES: CHANGE AND CONTINUITY

Healthy stories give guidance about developmental needs and the nature of change. This change process involves growth which is marked by times of upheaval or radical change and subsequent periods of relative stability. The interrelated processes of change and continuity are characterized by a creative (yet often stressful) balance. This process of interwoven change and then stabilization also occurs in every developmental model (e.g. cognitive, moral, psychosocial) valued by psychology. Rollo May, in his book *The Courage to Create,* says that the secret of creative works (art, literature, music), just like creative lives and loves, is a balance of form and passion.

> Limiting and expanding go together. In the creative act the boundaries of our world shift under our feet and we tremble while waiting to see whether any new form will take the place of the lost boundary or whether we can create some new order out of this chaos. As imagination gives vitality to form, form keeps imagination from driving us crazy.
> —Rollo May, *The Courage to Create*

In a thoughtful book by Cox and Theilgaard (1987), it is suggested that a psychotherapist can enable another person to "melt into the foreground" of his own life (p. 222). Important life events help us recall the larger story and to periodically ask, "What kind of story am I in? am I creating?"

Similarly, in their book *Rituals for Our Times,* Imber-Black and Roberts (1992, pp. 23–56) emphasize that rituals provide ways to transform feelings, beliefs and relationships. Rituals help storylines make sense whether the climate is clear or chaotic. They offer five purposes for ritual: (1) relating, via shaping, expressing and maintaining relationships; (2) changing, via making and marking transitions; (3) healing, via recovery from betrayal, trauma or loss; (4) believing, via voicing convictions and making meaning and (5) celebrating, via affirming joy and honoring life with festivity. Rituals help us recognize who we are, who we have been and who we can become. Rituals can give us an interactive and vital human landscape for roots and wings.

Living our stories and telling our meaning is the creative challenge to preserve an ageless self. Reformation, redirection and renewed meaning help balance an identity across our lifespan. The interest and availability of caring listeners (community, friends, family or caregivers) who will hear the *end tale* honors both the teller and the listener. This story tending preserves the hard-won wisdom across generations, an honoring and honorable pursuit.

> All things and all (people) call on us with small or loud voices. They want us to listen, they want us to understand their intrinsic claims, their justice of being. But we can give it to them only through the love that listens.
> —Paul Tillich, *Love, Power and Justice*

5

Story Tending: Leit Motifs, Hunches, Hopes and Fears

T. Peake and S. Rosenzweig

Psychology has rediscovered an old truth. The old truth is that stories of people's lives can be healing, entertaining, tragic and redeeming. Psychology also has a growing literature on the use of narrative in understanding people's inner workings and on using narrative, oral history and storytelling to help people heal and grow psychologically. Unfortunately, most of the psychology literature on this topic is not a very interesting story. The literature is usually couched in the stilted and, at times, baffling language of medical and social scientists. The best balance would be scholarly ideas (on how life stories define, direct and heal people) blended with good literature. This personal literature includes gripping reflections, poetry and quotes.

In this chapter we consider core dimensions of narrative wisdom. The first principle is that people develop and preserve identity through individual life stories. Valuable scholarly works on this topic include those by Linda Viney (1993), Sharon Kaufman (1986), Josselson and Lieblich (1993) and G. S. Howard (1991), to name a few. Moving beyond the scholarly ideas, we will sample gripping reflections and motifs of real people. Some quotes help set the stage. Then hunches, the hopes and fears of average folks, are examined. We look first at core fears or "anxiety closets" and then at treasured hopes that propel us. By hunches, we mean those embedded conscious or unconscious convictions on which people bet their lives. These core motivations or *leitmotifs* unlock the secrets to past themes and future possibilities. While doing psychotherapy with people for more than twenty years, we have heard fascinating, shocking, sad and inspiring stories of how people act, why they say they act that way and what they believe is crucial in life. The hunches often change or are reformed at different life stages. People bet their lives on these hunches. These beliefs are often the best place to hunt for pathos, problems and life revisions.

> Paradox is what turns novelists on. Linear valor is not as important to them as light and shade.
> —Thomas Kineally (Author of *Shindler's List*)

Willa Cather suggested, "There are only two or three human stories, and they go on repeating themselves as fiercely as if they never happened before." Perhaps she is right that there are only two or three themes that send currents through everyone's lives. However it seems that the variations on those themes and the beliefs and convictions that guide people's lives are many. The stories are sometimes tragic, sometimes funny, sometimes inspired, but mostly entertaining.

> Should we all confess our sins to one another, we would all laugh at one another for our lack of originality.
> —Kahlil Gibran

> Nothing is so burdensome as a secret.
> —French proverb

> All sorrows can be borne if you put them into a story or tell a story about them.
> —Isak Dinesen

As already mentioned, Sharon Kaufman (1986) has given us a profound suggestion. She urges us to honor people by helping them tell and modify their life stories. Being able to know oneself (what we value, what we have done, who we love and why) is the backbone of creating and preserving an identity through life. People's life stories convey a conviction with a pattern, a plan or a life bet of sorts.

Art is a kind of confession. All artists if they are to survive, are forced at last to tell the whole story; to purge the anguish up.
   —James Baldwin

I've learned that in the course of our life we leave and are left and let go of much that we love. Losing is the price we pay for living. It is also the source of much of our growth and gain.
   —Judith Viorst, *Necessary Losses*

Irony is the ability to look at yourself clearly and still get the joke.

What logic can't grasp metaphor can. Metaphor is the hand thrust under the water catching live fish. Metaphor is a passageway between fantasy and logic; it will take you someplace new.
   —Blanche McCrary Boyd, *The Redneck Way*
   of Knowledge

Parenthetically we would like to offer one caution. Life stories are not always entertaining; they can be dull, inarticulate and underwhelming. Our plea in this book, for narrative paths to healing and growth, could backfire. If we romanticize life stories too much we may miss the importance of modest and less articulate lives. The lives of poor storytellers may need hearing the most.

HOPES AND FEARS

This chapter is about narrative wisdom and telling stories. This section considers bedrock motives—the hopes and fears that guide, drive or inspire people to live their lives a certain way. We focus on the beliefs on which people bet their lives, the hunches that shape their stories. We will actually only deal with fractions of those stories. It seems that often a core belief, fear or hope encapsulates the theme of a person's story, a belief that shapes one's life. In counseling people of every age, but especially more vividly with older adults, we have the opportunity to hear people candidly "think out loud." In this atmosphere of trust but emotional honesty and urgency, we are sometimes privy to their root fears and their root beliefs, the gamble on which they bet their lives. In order to capture the range of these beliefs, we have included a number of short summaries or aphorisms (not always eloquent or articulate) that unveil these hopes and fears. Some of these short-quote encapsulations really do convey the essential plot or motive for people's lives. In therapy, we often help people search for patterns in their behavior. The patterns make more sense if we can discern their motives. In their narratives, we search for stories and motives that explain and account for the way lives are lived.

We call these beliefs *hunches.* They may be conscious or unconscious. While these hunches may be a vehement and rabid driving force at one stage of a person's life, the motives or core hunches often change at a later life stage. With older adults very often the wisest kind of hunches are those where an earlier belief was reconsidered and a newer vantage or conviction rules a later stage of life. Motives and perspectives may change at different eras of life.

> Old paint on canvas, as it ages, sometimes becomes transparent. When that happens it is possible, in some pictures to see the original lines: a tree will show through a woman's dress, a child makes way for a dog, a larger boat is no longer on an open sea. That is called pentimento because the painter "repented," changed his mind. Perhaps it would be as well to say that the old conception replaced by a later choice, is a way of seeing and then seeing again. The paint has aged now and I want to see what was there for me once, what is there for me now.
> —Lillian Hellman, *Pentimento*

As therapists it is our job to help people make creative changes in their *assumptive worlds* (Frank and Frank, 1991). We must listen to their peculiar tongues; to their prized hunches. People bet their lives on hunches. These convictions are wise, stupid, profane, tragic, grotesque and hilarious. The hunches are witting and unwitting. They are articulate and obscure. They are spoken and they are acted. Understanding these motives gives us choices about when or how to redirect our lives.

Anxiety Closets—Fears (Related to Developmental Needs)

People often stop being creative because they are stressed, afraid or anxious. There is even a term in psychopathology, the *neurotic paradox*, which describes this temporary stupidity. This paradox plays out behaviorally in the following way. In attempting to solve a conflicted situation, or deal with repeated emotional challenge, we often act in illogical or self-defeating ways. The neurotic paradox suggests that at a time when we are most challenged and we need to be the most flexible, we are probably the least creative. Rather than respond flexibly in such a pressured situation, we act in the same repetitive way we always have. We repeat old patterns in a kind of urgent stereotyped way of behaving. Creativity is scarce because the stress or urgency is so extreme. People are driven by these fears as much as they are by their hopes, and they are often more the hostage of fears than a shaper of their fates. Prominent fears we have encountered include the following.

Worried I'll be:
- old
- poor
- abandoned-isolated-lonely
- ridiculed/humiliated
- found out (impostor)
- vulnerable-unsafe
- overestimated
- unloved
- unappreciated
- useless
- damned
- finite
- purposeless
- impotent
- harmed
- powerless
- overwhelmed (conquered)

> Worry often gives a small thing a big shadow.
> —Swedish proverb

Hunches and Hopes (Betting Your Life)

Some people are emphatic, if not articulate, about what they feel is important in actions, beliefs or relations. These hunches are sometimes very complex. However, listening to a person's life story or episodes of her life generally reveals a common core theme. A recurrent pattern or motive emerges. One of the fascinating things about psychotherapy is watching patterns crystallize and repeat themselves. Part of the benefit of therapy is pointing out hidden patterns or blind spots in one's behavior. Sometimes people know very clearly what their hunches or hopes are, and other times they may be the last to know. What follows are a collection of aphorisms, mottoes or axioms that propel a person's efforts. These beliefs are entertaining, shocking, enlightening and sometimes freeing.

This section presents quotes about people's motives. Prominently intertwined are memorable hunches on which we have heard people bet their lives. These short stories or more accurately, these phrases, mottoes or cryptic beliefs, are drawn from an array of friends, acquaintances, families and patients whom we have known.

In order to set the tone, we consider the following combination of quotes from well-known individuals.

> By reaching out of psychology and into literature with an eye to common sense and plain language, we aim to loosen the soil that has buried the story of (human) experience, removing the thatch of a mystifying language in order to see what grows.
> —Bruno Bettelheim, *The Uses of Enchantment*

> You are a good man Duffy but you are willful. I got a feeling that you missed a whole lot of good things in your life because you decided too much ahead of time.
> —Harry Crews, *All We Need Of Hell*

> The important thing is to be well-liked.
> — Willy Loman, in *Death of a Salesman*

> One of the symptoms of an approaching nervous breakdown is the belief that one's work is terribly important.
> —Bertrand Russell

> I want to beg you, as much as I can, to be patient toward all that is unsolved in your heart and try to love the questions themselves. Do not seek answers that can be given you by another because you would not be able to live another's answers. And the point is, to live everything. Live the ques-

tions now. Perhaps you will then gradually without noticing it, live along some distant day into the answer.
> —Rainer Maria Rilke

Aging calls us outdoors (after the adult indoors of work- and love-life and keeping stylish), into the lowly simplici- ties that we thought we had outgrown as children. We come again to love the plain world. What a glorious view.
> —John Updike

Old men ought to be explorers here and there does not matter. We must be still and still moving into another in- tensity. For a further union a deeper communion through the dark cold and the empty desolation. In my end is my beginning.
> —T.S. Eliot

The following two selections contrast men and women's hunches about which is more important—relationship or achievement. Excerpts from James Joyce and Carol Gilligan highlight an apparent gender difference.

> —What then is your point of view? Cranly asked. His last phrase, sour smelling as the smoke of charcoal, excited Stephen's (Daedalus) brain over which its fumes seemed to brood.
> —Look here, Cranly, he said. You have asked me what I would do and what I would not do. I will tell you. I will not serve in that which I no longer believe whether it call it- self my home, my fatherland or my church; and I will try to express myself in some mode of life or art as freely as I can and as wholly as I can, using for my defence the only arms I allow myself to use—silence, exile, and cunning.
> —Cunning indeed! (Cranly said). Is it you? You poor poet you!
>> —James Joyce, A Portrait of the Artist as a
>> Young Man

For Stephen (Daedalus), leaving childhood meant renuncia- tion of relationships in order to protect his freedom of self expression. For (many women) "farewell to childhood" means relinquishing the freedom of self-expression in order

to protect others and preserve relationships. These divergent constructions of identity, in self expression or in self-sacrifice, create different problems for (gender and human) development—the former a problem of human connection, and the latter a problem of truth. These seemingly disparate problems, however, are intimately related. Men's return from exile and silence parallels women's return from equivocation, until intimacy and truth converge in the discovery of the connection between integrity and care.
—Carol Gilligan (on Joyce's protagonist
Stephen) *In a Different Voice*

If these two quotes are too cryptic the interested reader will find the works of Daniel Levinson (*The Seasons of a Man's Life*, 1978, and *The Seasons of a Woman's Life*, 1996) a valuable elaboration of the contrasting values of relatedness versus achievement in women and men's psychosocial development.

Hunches (Leitmotifs, Developmental Stages and Folks We Know)

Consider the following array of personal adages or hunches we have run across in therapy and other conversations.

Dan   Live fast, love hard, die young.

Dan came from a proud and upstanding family who traced their recent roots back four generations working for the same utility company. Dan had been sent to Vietnam as a helicopter pilot, experiencing the most nightmarish scenes and situations anyone could live through. Dan was trying to make sense of his life and was having a difficult time. In the return to his former home after these combat experiences, Dan lived with a cavalier flair, denying any sentimentality. He had also picked up a way of coping in Southeast Asia which included hashish and other sundry "combat medication." When his cavalier facade cracked, he rented a plane and flew with his dog across one end of the state to the other. Dan was hospitalized and, once clear of his altered state of consciousness, was shortly back to his old self. He was a charmer with an infectious bravado and sense of humor; however, he was haunted. His motto was "live fast, love hard, and die young." His motto was haunting him now. He had not died young as had many of his friends in the war. At the same time he was happy to be home with his family, but bristled at the "oppressive weight of my family's expectations" that he should join the same company where all the men in his family had worked. However, his crystallized motto became the handle he used to control, understand and direct himself. We were able to use that adage metaphorically. He likened it to a source of power for him, not unlike the power controls of the gun helicopter he flew in combat. He told of how dangerous and intricate the "Huey" was to fly. He had a fierce pride and respected that control lever. Over time he explained, as he came to understand it, that lever, that source of energy, could also needlessly be the end of him. He said the quote gave him energy in the past, but now gave him a deep sadness and confusion. Those friends with whom he shared the idea had not all made it home—they did die young. Would he be disloyal to change his motto?

Lilly   Leave it lay where Jesus flung it.

Lilly was a spitfire. She vacillated between being a little too proper and a little too bawdy. It was an entertaining swing. However Lilly was widowed not too long ago. She had shared an active, challenging and joyful life with her husband, the only man she really loved. In the last few years, she had taken a more passive role as his wife. She told stories about the times before her marriage. She had grown up in the "fancier parts of the Appalachian Mountains." She had a lilting southern accent and an explosive ironic sense of humor, with a knack for puncturing stodgy traditions of "landed gentry."

Earlier in her life Lilly had studied acting at a well-known acting school in New York. She learned to love the theater and the high energy atmosphere of music, drama and "the best the bards have to offer."

More recently, she criticized herself for having become dependent and having trouble remaking her life after her husband died. She would rail and rage about injustices and be angry at her own dependence, which seemed to have "sprung up when she wasn't looking." She vacillated between a deep sadness and inertia often followed by waves of high energy and extravagance. She overwhelmed her friends and acquaintances with high-energy courses of action that were short on caution and short on planning. *Mood swings* is the prosaic way medicine might describe it.

After a number of conversations with her, she told the writer that things "sure would have gone a lot faster in therapy" if only the therapist had known better how to tell her to "calm down" and not try to change everything. She said if something can't be changed, "Leave it lay where Jesus flung it." This was a kind of mantra that she had to tell herself when she was feeling too driven and urgent, interfering and actually self-defeating. We have used her quote often because it applies to many people. Lilly also insisted that the same sentiment was at the core of the philosophy of twelve-step programs such as Alcoholics Anonymous. A memorable life hunch indeed.

Jean and Gary   Healing the memories heals the present, past and future.

As we came to know Jean, she had been struggling with a bone-splintering form of cancer. After it was diagnosed it attacked her for more than ten years Jean and Gary had been married for more than forty years. She came for counseling for herself and for the couple. For herself, she wanted to talk about various experimental treatments she had considered. She also sought pain management to soften the ravages of both the disease itself and the side effects of conventional chemo and radiation treatments. She taught the listener an important lesson about the need to sort through her life's emotional attic and finish unfinished business. For the couple, she and Gary wanted to have a safe place to talk about their feelings, their own sadness, their own relationship, and their plan for the aftermath of her imminent death.

Throughout the physical assault she experienced, Jean looked for medications that could minimize the pain but not cloud her thoughts nor her sense of self. In dabbling with less proven procedures or alternative treatments for cancer (which generated new sources of hope), she pursued them with an appropriate skepticism and even a sense of humor. She was as clear about realizing her own need for a new hope as she was clear in her sense of humor about some of the silliness she encountered in various treatment centers (such as one that helped modify her aura).

The most important part of her treatment involved the therapist just listening and following her lead. This was her task of readdressing unfinished emotional issues. These included family, children and Gary. Between the pain, the treatments and this last task, her energy was taxed and waning. However, as the listener helped her select and then address the unresolved conflicts or troubling memories, we witnessed a powerful process of closure and serenity. Jean pursued these unfinished vignettes with a clarity of purpose that gave rise in each instance to a visible emotional release and resolution.

Gary supported Jean's emotional healing project. He also began to realize that a healing process for him had also begun. The love between them was inspiring. When death finally released Jean from the racking pain, a serenity accompanied Gary's sadness.

Gary stayed in touch on a regular basis. He struggled with the void her passing left, but he was able to maintain a focus. He often described his confidence that the efforts they made to talk about their past together and their future plans created a comfort in the face of sorrow. Gary later told me that on the anniversary of Jean's death he sat down with their family album and walked himself through pictures, the settings and the memories of their life together. He said that the difficult but important time they had spent, "finishing things" before Jean's death, helped him fully appreciate the value of *healing memories*.

Jack   Pursue art, ignore politics.

Jack was an interesting fellow—an artist and a musician as well as a teacher. He told how surprisingly easy the first forty years of his life had been. He knew he was gifted and had been tapped as a prodigy to train as a concert musician. The surprising ease of his success was heightened by his working class family background. He thrived on his creative talents and his creative power. He shared his aggravation, however, of having to deal with the politics, structure and practicalities that a musician encounters. Working with other musicians of equal or larger egos, dealing with community art councils that fund and schedule artistic efforts, plus having a family whose needs interfered with his unbridled creative pursuits were his vexing aggravations.

By the time the listener entered his life, Jack felt his creative forces compromised by the "revenge of colleagues who envied my talents and resented my natural gifts." These gifts were wrapped in an egocentric package. Jack talked about how things had probably come too easily. He was stumped by complications in his children's lives. Life was not flowing as easily in the past fifteen years, as during the first fifty years. He was failing in finances and relationships. The burden was overwhelming his wife as well. His role in the symphony was being challenged in a coup to unseat him. Also in his role as a music professor, his colleagues were fed up with the "prima donna," who had tormented them so long.

Jack's motto had worked for many years. Now it was failing. In our conversations, he raged and railed at the unfairness of his plight. His anger spewed until it turned into depression. At that point, our conversation moved in a different direction, one that considered a new approach to this phase in his life. He was able to accomplish this reconsideration. He was able to redirect his creative talents and his belief in music in new roles. He started to learn the art of consideration in relating to his children and wife. Jack made changes for the latter years of his life. As a result, his teaching and artistic ability formed new arenas, new students and new audiences. Humility and consideration of others become valuable ingredients in his hunches about life.

Randy   Life is like a shit sandwich. The more bread you
                   got, the less shit you gotta eat.

Randy was a salesman. He had grown up in a family where his parents toiled long hours and long years to earn a life of honest but meager existence. He recalled going to school in clean but modest clothes often handed down from cousins or the families in households where his mother was a cleaning woman. His father worked a small farm owned by someone else. Randy carried this resentful sense of inferiority and anger at his parents for his low place "in the food chain of life." When the listener came to know him, he had reached a point of extreme suspicion and isolation from others. He had been ruthlessly effective in business dealings and purchase negotiations. His lasting anger channeled into the belief that people respected only money, power and financial success.

Randy's current dilemma was his powerful belief in the saying above, which he was using to guide his life. His struggle was whether to contend with his increasing suspiciousness and sense of isolation and retain this powerful belief, or to reconsider his hunch. He had been successful in sales and in deals across a lifetime. As his adage suggests, he believed that everybody's task was the same but that the task could be made easier by wealth and whatever power went along with it. Occasionally, his sense of humor would reappear in the midst of his dilemmas. He would laugh that at least he was still able to pack his lunch.

Ethel   Stay away from them doctors, they can kill you.

Ethel was a noble woman of modest means, with a deep love for family and a disarming sense of humor. Ethel had outlived four husbands. She sometimes joked that "they just don't make them like they used to." She had been a cook for many years in several cafes and diners in the Midwest. Now, long since retired and settled in a rural community, she was surrounded by grandchildren and a wide circle of friends she had made over the years.

The toughest struggle of her life, she said, was that all of her children had died before her. She did rejoice, however, "that I'm surrounded with grandchildren and great grandchildren."

Her funny and inspiring reflection about staying away from doctors, however, was always worth a cleansing belly laugh. Although her resolve to stay away from them doctors was based on the sadness of her children's death, it may have been prophetic. Perhaps Ethel knew the peculiar and iatrogenic directions that our health care system can take.

Karl   The power is with the gatekeeeper. Dress British
                     and think Yiddish.

Karl had a long and successful career in the government. He worked in high-level security and intelligence. He had grown up in a broken home with a mother who had many partners and pursued her own life, leaving Karl to generally fend for himself. He mentioned on numerous occasions that he trusted no one, and he learned to rely on his own wits and resourcefulness. He was an educated and intelligent man who learned much about personnel selection and the psychological makeup of others. This was his stock in trade in international intelligence and the U.S. Foreign Service. He was adept at gaining power and influence by the intriguing specialty of understanding the motives and personality of others. This skill, along with his top security clearance, allowed him to be "the gatekeeper." He was able to decide who would be excluded from this secretive, exciting, yet exclusive fraternity. He was able to influence decisions about who was the enemy of our country. Karl liked being in the position of knowing vast amounts of information about others and using his leverage to exclude or one-up them.

Karl would reminisce fondly about the glamour of being treated like a head of state as he worked in different countries as an honored consultant. He loved the special favors that went along with his position and also the fear his position engendered in others. He also prided himself on being able to move in and out of different cultures, different countries and different customs. His secret to his success he attributed to this advice, "Dress British and think Yiddish."

Rita   Do unto others before they do unto you.
                 Payback's a bitch.

Rita had sought inpatient psychological help, uncertain whether she was doing it merely as a diversion (to shake legal authorities who were after her and her family) or whether she really was psychiatrically troubled. Once we began to talk, it became clear that she was frightened about past wounds and demons. Put another way, Rita came for treatment to fool us and to hide. However, she was afraid she was fooling herself, and she desperately needed a place to safely clear out her personal attic of suspicion, con games, violence and victimization. Her family had been involved in organized crime and had apparently been very successful in this frightening business.

Rita had lived a life she both loved and hated. Eventually, she was able to overcome her suspicion and share hair-raising stories of betrayal, fortune and brutal violence. She was also surprised that she was "living to a riper old age than I ever expected."

In the early part of our conversations, she would often press to ensure that her listener was not carrying a weapon. When this came as a surprise to the therapist, she shared her belief that one should follow a different version of the golden rule, "Do unto others before they do unto you." She had other phrases expressing a similar sentiment. "Payback's a bitch," was another intensely focusing hunch that guided her thoughts and actions. In spite of her skeptical and hypervigilant approach to life (apparently well-founded in the culture she was raised), she had a sense of humor that allowed her to laugh at herself. It took her a long time to feel comfortable enough to explore some of her nightmares and to confess crimes done to and by her. She remained cautious but began some healing in a safe relation.

Barbara   Be nice to everyone. You meet the same
                    people going up as you do coming down.

Barbara was a joy to be around. She had raised a family of four children and had accomplished it with the same husband with whom she had begun. She had also worked outside the home as an administrative assistant (she reminded the listener that it was called a secretary in her day) for a variety of businesses. She prided herself on being able to make a boss look a lot smarter than he actually was. In moments of honesty, with closest friends, she would also admit that she could put the career whammy on an inconsiderate young executive if need be in order to teach him a lesson.
Barbara's comforting and focused hunch was, "Be nice to everyone. You meet the same people going up as you do coming down."

Malcolm   Don't mistake kindness for weakness.

Malcolm, whom the listener knew in the army, grew up in times of racial troubles and tensions. Working alongside someone doing jobs (anywhere along the spectrum from mundane to cruel to frightening) creates a window to see "what people are made of." The military throws people together from different cultures and social strata, and we knew Malcolm at a time when hatred ran deep between southern whites and blacks emerging from oppression, fear and misunderstanding.
In spite of these times, Malcolm was accesible regardless of our different races. More surprisingly, he ignored pressure from his "home boys" to drop our friendship. There was a quiet confidence about him. He was admired by anyone who could see past racial stereotypes. Probably part of his secret was an adaptive sense of humor. He could point out sham, false pride, selfish motives and cruelty in others in a way that created explosive laughter rather than explosive conflict.

On one occasion, however, he was sent to purchase supplies for his platoon. Upon his return, he began passing out provisions to the men. Overhearing his conversation with one of his black compatriots, he realized the other man was accusing him of cheating. Malcolm was accused of not delivering and the accuser of not paying what he owed. His usual joking ability to puncture confrontation was not working. The accuser would not come across with what he owed. Threats were made. The usually easy-going Malcolm grabbed the man and pinned him against a fence. "Don't ever mistake kindness for weakness," was the riveting warning he issued.

This phrase captured the way Malcolm wished to live his life. He valued kindness and honesty. He did not want to fight, especially in the war we were trained for, but neither would he shrink in the face of injustice. In subsequent years we are told Malcolm's phrase found its way into a popular song. We hope the sentiment could find its way into popular usage.

Hank   Someone's gonna pay and it ain't going to be me.

Hank was injured on the job four years ago and has been struggling with chronic back pain since then. He had previously been diagnosed with congestive heart failure and cardiomyopathy. He expected that after his back surgery, he would be "perfectly well" but has had a long, slow and difficult recuperation. Hank met his second wife, Phyllis, dancing about ten years ago. He was a mild mannered man, whom Phyllis described as "sweet and fun." As Hank's health deteriorated, however, his wife commented that "I don't know who he is any longer." Hank, in his mid-60s, has been forced to confront Erikson's later stage, *Integrity versus Despair*, without having worked through the prior stages. After several failed marriages, he finally found Phyllis, but as a result of his rages and tantrums he was pushing her out of the house. Hank hoped to be enjoying the end of his working years and looking out for his family (and stepfamily). Instead, he was mostly homebound and dependent on disability payments to make ends meet. As the years since his back surgery passed and his heart weakened, Hank became more angry and intolerant of his wife's friends. He demanded that Phyllis and her daughters take care of him, and he constantly raged at the misfortunes dealt to him. Struggling to maintain an intimate connection with Phyllis while simultaneously attempting to confront the last months of his life, Hank had been looking back on his life and despairing over what he had created. His motto that "someone's gonna pay" was haunting him. His family was withdrawing from his anger as it created the isolation he feared most. As noted in the previous chapter, sometimes the stories at this life juncture are anguished rather than inspiring.

The next cluster of fifteen hunches was such an unusual discovery it begged to be included in this section. The quotes are engraved on a marble bench by the Boston Park Plaza, observed at the 1990 American Psychological Association Convention

1. A strong sense of duty imprisons you.
2. Absolute submission can be a form of freedom.
3. Artificial desires are despoiling the earth.
4. Drama often obscures the real issues.
5. Elaboration is a form of pollution.
6. In some instances it is better to die than continue.
7. It's better to be a good person than a famous person.
8. Myths make reality more intelligible.
9. Often you should act like you are sexless.
10. Talking is used to hide one's inability to act.
11. The idea of revolution is an adolescent fantasy.
12. When something terrible happens, people wake up.
13. You are guileless in your dreams.
14. Being alone with yourself is increasingly unpopular.
15. Exceptional people deserve special concessions.

—Anonymous

Not knowing whose thoughts these were, it is interesting to speculate about his or her motives and background.

Mother Teresa   "We can do no great things only small
                          things with great love."

We did not have the pleasure of meeting Mother Teresa, but we felt the above quote was an elegant closing example of a hunch that guides someone's life and motives while touching others.

THERAPEUTIC IMPLICATIONS

One might ask, "Why the brief adages? Why these central quotes?" After hearing these hunches emerge in interviews with older adults, we discovered the practical limitations of listening to another's life story. At a workshop on "Telling Stories" given by the senior author, a woman asked this question, "Once you get these folks started talking, how do you get them to stop?" It would be nice if we could all count on having a listener who could listen as long as we needed to talk. Perhaps that option is what makes friendships so important. We often notice that an older adult isolated by the loss of a friend or partner is hungry for a chance to let the memories unravel with a caring listener. If they are really needy, then there are lots of stories to tell. Be advised. Telling one's story is an attempt to persuade the teller as well as the listener. When there is an outpouring of memories, the teller's search for meaning is made possible through an audience or a jury. Hearing another person tell her life meaning, hope or fear helps the teller to understand herself. This clear, short hunch is a manageable insight, a manageable motive, rather than a rambling searching account "looking for its own meaning." The succinct summary of a story or hunch makes it easier to grasp the person's central guiding beliefs. By making motives and problems clearer, people can understand faulty assumptions and change their life stories.

When counseling older adults, hunches help clarify core problems (a core dynamic) and help create core solutions. Skill in discerning these pivotal beliefs and patterns helps a therapist get to the heart of the life story, modify it when needed and keep the therapy process as short as possible. Managed health care companies like that brevity and efficiency. More importantly, skill in hearing the crucial life theme helps us practice the *minimal interference principle* (Segal, 1964). That principle demands that we make the least amount of change necessary. At first, it might seem that our plea to hear the individual's whole life story contradicts the goal of finding succinct anecdotes or aphorisms tht define a person. On the contrary, the two tasks work well together to ensure a realistic balance between ethical care and limited resources. The minimal interference principle is a way to minimize change and maximize continuity.

We hope to deal with only the necessary losses that propel psychological growth throughout the lifespan. That ability—to hear and extract core themes or root hopes and fears—provides a vehicle to make only minor changes in a life story rather than take on a task of reconstruction. We can honor the individual's whole story. However, change happens best when we focus on fulcrum patterns, beliefs, actions and motivations. This strategy works by helping people rediscover and modify old solutions and strategies to fit current difficulties. This principle is a way of preserving a person's identity while retaining and building on hardwon experience and wisdom. Storytelling and story tending represent a vital force needed to promote and preserve healthy aging. The minimal interference principle adds an elegant, efficient and transforming skill.

TELLING ONE'S TALE—STANDARD AND REVISED VERSIONS

> What we must decide is perhaps how we are valuable rather than how valuable we are.
> —Edgar Z. Friedenberg

The life story examples we used focused on condensed versions. In a recent article, Haim Omer (1993) has described a highly condensed psychobiography as a way to focus and shorten the counseling process. In his interesting account, he uses a central issue or theme to focus a core dynamic in therapy. At times he caricatures that central theme, core behavior pattern or belief. Helping crystallize this core hunch, fear or conviction helps a person see what he or she values, and helps to rethink a hunch that is wrong or outmoded. Perhaps the technique can show an irony and enable a gentle laugh at one's own expense. We have tried to characterize some of the hunches or beliefs that shape and drive different people's lives, and we hope we have not given the impression that these convictions or private stories are inflexible. Crystallizing these core patterns is a means to heal and reshape life stories. What the heart knows today, the head may understand tomorrow.

Recognizing the worries, convictions and hunches that guide our lives allows us to keep what is good and change what is problematic. The telling of life stories (or life sketches, caricatures or epithets) is not just an intellectual process. The stories have blood coursing through their veins. They are emotional as well as thoughtful.

An important process responsible for a great portion of the healing value of psychotherapy is the concept of a *corrective emotional experience.* Such an experience involves three dimensions. One of them is the ability to describe the situation —what is going on. A clear understanding of a pattern or dynamic is a way of "naming the demon." A second dimension of a corrective emotional experience is the emotional landscape or backdrop that fosters or provokes a pattern of behavior. Understanding the emotional trigger or the implicit history that first prompted this way of acting is crucial. The third dimension calls for a new and improved ending to an old pattern or story. The old way of relating, which served a valuable function earlier in one's life, is no longer adequate for new life demands. This third dimension writes a revised plot or a new ending for the emotional puzzles and behavior patterns of earlier times.

It would be a mistake to think that the hunches that guide one's life at one time cannot be altered at another life phase. Helping a person express, listen to and shape a sense of self and direction is good art, good friendship and good treatment. Sometimes this process involves looking at aspects of the story that have been forgotten. The notion of healing painful memories takes place in therapy but can also occur outside of therapy with the right combination of understanding, encouragement and respect.

Telling stories and narrative wisdom flow from hunches—hopes and fears. Beliefs and self tales need to be stabilized and clarified for reflection and direction. Throughout the lifespan there are periods of relative stabilization and periods of change. Therefore, the most inspiring life stories tell us how to preserve a stable sense of self in times of too much change, yet an ability to grow and change when the old sense of self is stagnant.

NOTE

Susan G. Rosenzweig, Psy.D. is a private practice psychologist in Portland, Oregon.

6

Healing and Illness Stories

Stories about illness and attitudes about healing offer a human slant on medical illnesses and syndromes. Arthur Kleinman, a psychiatrist and professor of anthropology at Harvard University compiled an interesting book called *The Illness Narratives: Suffering, Healing and the Healing Condition* (1988). Dr. Kleinman sets a different tone to understand the personal experience of illness. By *illness* he means something fundamentally different from disease. "By invoking the term illness, I mean to conjure up the innately human experience of symptoms and suffering. Illness refers to how the sick person and the members of the family perceive, live with, and respond to symptoms and disability" (Kleinman, 1988, p. 3). Illness involves the experience of symptoms such as cramps or a painful joint. Illness also includes categorizing and explaining in commonsense ways the kinds of distress caused by a disease. Kleinman values the patient's judgments about how best to cope with distress and the practical problems that accompany illness. For example, illness behavior consists of beliefs about aiding treatment, such as changing diet, resting, exercising, taking nonprescription medication or even following doctors' orders. Disease-related disability creates illness problems that change the way we live our lives. One may not be able to walk upstairs to the bedroom. A person may feel great anger because no one can see the pain and therefore other people think the disability is not real. Illness may bring demoralization and a loss of hope of getting better.

The healer (whatever his health profession) interprets illness in a taxonomy or a disease nosology; this name labels the disease. The disease is the problem from the practitioner's perspective, whereas the illness is the disease from the patient's and family's perspective. This distinction is important because the way a patient describes, understands and casts the illness deeply affects the outcome. What follows are examples of how attitude about disease or illness affects the healing process.

The story is told of working in a dialysis center for patients with chronic kidney disease. A *double-bind* conflict situation is created by the conflicting roles patients are asked to take and the roles by which physicians can be handcuffed. Patients in this kidney dialysis unit were first urged to be independent, not passive and dependent, "and be active in your care, but when you have a serious exacerbation, place yourself submissively in your doctor's hands, and we will blame you for what you did or what you failed to do to worsen your disorder" (Kleinman, 1988, pp. 170). The two conflicting role demands disorient patients and create guilt feelings. Guilt most certainly can interfere with care and the expectations of getting better.

The writer worked as a consulting psychologist on an acute physical rehabilitation unit of a general hospital. The active role demands placed on patients in such units have a positive effect. In contrast, patients on the other medical-surgical floors are cast in the familiar passive patient role. The patient lies and waits for medication, IV tubes, transportation to lab or diagnostic imaging procedures, and tries to catch precious minutes with the doctor to find out what is going on. People are transferred to a physical rehabilitaion unit after medical stabilization from an accident, surgery or acute episode. The attitude on this unit is to rapidly restrengthen, retrain and reactivate the patient. Accordingly the patient is immediately put in the role of being as physically and psychologically as active as possible. Often patients call their PT (physical therapist) their "physical torturer," in a grudging but fond combination of meanings. Not only the physical therapist but everyone on the unit pushes people to do everything that they can, to be active in their own recovery. Patients on such units have sustained spinal cord injuries, head injuries, amputations and other injuries or diseases that require extended rehabilitation to optimize recovery. Not surprisingly, depression accompanies the physical losses and debilitating injuries or diseases that these people experience. An active and involved patient role is essential for hope and recovery. Patients are not allowed to focus on the illness but are instead forced into an active and self-directed role as quickly and persistently as possible. This active role combats depression and serves as an antidote for the passivity that can worsen a depression. This physically active approach creates an "incidental potency" in treating the depression that accompanies physical injury. The social context of the illness, then, is a different story from the taxonomy of disease. To ignore this broader context would needlessly compromise healing and recovery (see also Kaufman and Becker, 1991).

Perhaps there is some comfort in Kleinman's (1988, p. 259) observation that most care for illness is delivered by the family rather than by medical professionals. It is with the family that symptoms are first discovered and finally cared for. Kleinman feels that viewing the patient as a colleague in therapy creates a collaboration that improves both the patient-doctor relationship and the quality of care. An attitudinal shift in medicine could develop paradigms of practice aimed at caring for a patient's illness needs rather than just treating disease symptoms (p. 265).

Another interesting source of healing stories and illness metaphors comes from a column in the *Journal of the American Medical Association*. Begun in 1980, this column, called *A Piece of My Mind*, includes essays, poems and even drawings. Physicians take the opportunity to divulge some of their most deeply held feelings and experiences in very human stories. At times the stories have a chilling honesty, at times an inspiring hopefulness.

One of the editors (Bruce B. Dan, 1988, pp. 92–93) of this column describes the concept of triage, which is a telling metaphor for health care.

Triage is a word you won't find in many dictionaries, but Doctors use it all the time, even though most of them don't know where it comes from. Tree-ahj, with the accent on the first syllable, means to direct patients to an appropriate area for medical care. The word is used both as a verb and as a noun, an actual place where such decisions are made. Few know that the term was first used by Napoleon's Surgeon General in an attempt to deal with the massive numbers of casualties suffered by the French troops during the Napoleonic wars. He decided to divide the wounded into three groups (hence the term triage): those whose wounds were so slight that they were not in need of immediate medical attention, those whose injuries were so severe that medical care would be of no use, and last those who would benefit from what little medicine had to offer at the turn of the nineteenth century.

Triage is also a revealing metaphor in the treatment of older adults. Decisions may be made that someone is beyond help; that someone has a truly acute condition and needs attention; or that someone's problem is so slight that it does not warrant medical care. Using the definitions from Kleinman, we could find illness anywhere in that trichotomy. Classification based on a triage medical model may run counter to the illness experience that families must face. That is why the essays in *A Piece of My Mind* strike a nice balance of physician as practitioner and physician as human being. Consider the following two excerpts from these essays.

Messages

Perhaps the fact that the great depression hit just as she and my father were starting out to raise their family had something to do with it, but no matter. Already as a small child I was aware that in the handling of money my mother was more than simply thrifty; she was down right frugal. Extravagances and luxuries did not exist. The one exception was a new, frilly, never-worn nightgown that she kept in the bottom drawer of the bureau. But even that had its purpose: "In case I should ever have to go into the hospital," she said. The nightgown lay there for years, carefully protected in its tissue wrappings.

But one day many years later the time came. The nightgown with its now yellowed lace and limp ruffles was taken from its wrappings and my mother entered a hospital seeking an answer to the mysterious fevers, sweats, and malaise that had plagued her life like a flu since autumn just before her 69th birthday.

We did not have long to wait for an answer. It came with the finality of a period at the end of a long sentence of strung out hyphenated clauses: Lymphoma, disseminated, regressive. Privately, her physician told me he was sorry, there was probably only a matter of two or three weeks left, certainly less than even a month.

For days I agonized over what to do with this information that only I had been told. Should I tell the family? should I tell my mother? did she already know? if not, did she suspect? could I talk with her? could I give her any hope? could I keep up any hope she might have? was there in fact any hope? Some relief came when I realized her birthday was approaching. The nightgown she had saved all those years she was now wearing, but it was hopelessly dated. I resolved to lift her spirits by buying her the handsomest and most expensive matching nightgown and robe I could find.

If I could not hope to cure her disease, at least I could make her feel like the prettiest patient in the entire hospital.

For a long time after she unwrapped her birthday present, given early so she would have longer to enjoy it, my mother said, "Would you mind returning it to the store? I really don't want it." Then she picked up the newspaper and turned to the last page. "This is what I really want, if you could get that," she said. What she pointed to was a display advertisement of expensive designer summer purses.

My reaction was one of disbelief. Why would my mother so careful about extravagances, want an expensive summer purse in January, one that she could not possibly use until June? She would not even live until spring, let alone summer. Almost immediately I was ashamed and appalled at my clumsiness, ignorance, insensitivity, call it what you will. With a shock I realized she was finally asking what I thought about her illness. She was asking me how long she would live. She was, in fact, asking me if I thought she would live even six months. And she was telling me that if I showed I believed she would live until then, then she would do it. She would not let that expensive purse go unused. That day I returned the gown and robe and bought the summer purse.

That was many years ago the purse is worn out and long gone, as are half a dozen others. And next week my mother flies to California to celebrate her 83rd birthday. Jane A. McAdams, M.D. (*A Piece of My Mind.* 1988, pp. 13–15).

A Second Opinion

Twenty years ago I was a medical resident. I remember one night I had seen three patients and none could be called interesting. Mr. Thomas was my fourth patient. His chief complaint was weakness. He had little spontaneity, his face was expressionless, his eyelids drooped, and his voice was nasal. My fatigue began to give way to excitement. Mr. Thomas was a very interesting patient. He answered yes to: do you ever see double? do you tire easily? do you have trouble swallowing? does food or water come back through your nose? has your voice changed? do your eyelids droop? Mr. Thomas was not impressed with the astuteness of my questions. If anything he became more apathetic. I had to strain to hear and understand him. "Mr. Thomas, I think I know what is wrong with you. I want to give you a small dose of medicine in the vein of your arm." The response to edrophonium chloride was dramatic. His eyelids flew open, he sat upright, his face was mobile, and his voice resonant. I could hardly contain myself. I had heard and read about myasthenia gravis, and I had diagnosed my first case all by myself. Mr. Thomas asked what disease I thought he had. "I believe you have a disease called myesthenia gravis. We will be able to help you." Something was wrong. The news seemed to sadden Mr. Thomas. He asked no questions about the disease or the treatment. The medication began to wear off. His eyelids drooped and his voice weakened. Mr. Thomas told me he knew he had mysthenia gravis. I was put out. "Why didn't you tell me? Why did you let me go through the history and give you Tensillon when you knew all the time what was wrong with you?" "I am sorry," he said. "I was hoping if I told you my symptoms, you—might diagnose something else, a disease you could cure. I take my medicine, but I am not doing well. I am afraid." Joseph E. Hardison, M.D. (*A Piece of My Mind*, 1988, pp. 80–81.)

The story of illness yearns to be a hopeful one, as seen in this gentleman's tragicomedy of hoping to find a doctor who would give him a better story, a better fate. The term *illness* has a way of personalizing and amplifying the too narrow concept of *disease.* For more recent examples of illness and healing stories the reader will find the book, *A Whole New Life, An Illness and a Healing* (Reynolds Price, 1994), a more complete acount of the personal tale of a life story reshaped by malady.

It is both humbling and humane to remember that most care for illness is delivered by family rather than health professionals. The person and family discover the symptoms first and care for them when the experts are gone. Viewing the patient as a colleague (whose attitude shapes the course of treatment) improves the quality of care.

The next chapter looks at illness, disease, treatment, and the systems of health care for older adults from the perspective of professionals who work with third agers (as well as what Baltes, 1997, describes as *fourth agers*). This Delphi research project compares and contrasts health care systems for the United States and the United Kingdom at the level of broad overview and personal perspectives. The results suggest a telling story or a troubling one at times. However, directions and considerations are discovered which can help write a healthier tale for balanced health care for older adults.

7

Health Care Systems in the United States and the United Kingdom: A Telling Story (A Delphi Comparison)

T. Peake, K. Sachs, R. Vidaver, C. Ballard and J. Rain

> As I see it, the chief concern of this generation has been
> the perfection of means, with a confusion of goals.
> —Albert Einstein

This chapter is guided by a conundrum. How difficult is it to balance informed and humane health care for older adults with limited resources and accessible services? Knowledge is often guided not so much by answering an initial question, but by discovering better, more answerable questions. What are the needs? What are the advantages or mistakes of past models? What are creative ways to find or support services in prevention, treatment and recovery? Are there places with good stories to tell about balancing the best health care with limited resources?

As part of a sabbatical on healthy aging and health care for older adults, the senior author (with Drs. Jeff Rain, Carol Ballard, Karl Sachs and Robert Vidaver) studied varieties and models of health and mental health care for seniors *(third agers)*. This research was supported by a variety of agencies, including a Tregaskis Bequest from the University of London, Florida Institute of Technology, Eastern Virginia Medical School, Tidewater Pastoral Counseling Center, Florida Mental Health Institute (Department of Aging and Mental Health), U.S. Navy Internship (Portsmouth, Va.), Pine Rest Christian Hospital,

Dartmouth/New Hampshire Hospital and the Prudence Skynner Family Therapy Clinic of Springfield Hospital and St. George's Hospital Medical School, London.

We completed parallel studies in the United States and the United Kingdom using a Delphi procedure that involved a repeated sampling of experts' opinions (modified by early results) about the needs and status of health care services for older adults. We sampled the caregivers' heartfelt expert opinions, in which they described health care as it is and how it ought to be, its ills and its needs. The first study was in the United States (1992–1994), and the second in the United Kingdom (1993–1995).

A summary of some of our research findings follows.

A DELPHI STUDY OF U.S. HEALTHCARE FOR THE ELDERLY: PROBLEMS, IMPEDIMENTS AND SOLUTIONS (STUDY 1)

Introduction

If there is any agreement on the subject of health care, it is that our present system has serious deficiencies. This is particularly true when considering health care for special populations such as the elderly. In order to improve health care for the elderly, we must first examine our beliefs about our elder citizens and how we got those beliefs.

Current American attitudes regarding old age (typically defined as age 65 and above) clearly reveal a decline in status of the elderly. Late life is generally regarded as a time of loss, declining physical health, deteriorating mental functioning and decreases in virtually all areas of life with few compensating gains. The old are often viewed as unattractive, sexless, passive, unproductive, dependent and ill.

These stereotypes linger despite ample evidence refuting them, and their pervasive influence can be felt in many areas of our society. Ageism, fusing the heterogeneous group of the elderly into a single image of "the old," has long affected policy on issues concerning the elderly. Professional health care providers, as members of the larger society, are not immune to cultural views and values regarding aging. If the problems associated with aging are seen as chronic, uncontrollable and inevitable, health care of the elderly is unlikely to make use of the same active, aggressive interventions used with younger individuals, even when all other relevant factors are equivalent. Aging may be seen incorrectly as the essential cause, resulting in other causes being discounted or dismissed.

The elderly are the fastest growing age group in America and by the year 2030 are expected to total 64 million, or approximately 20 percent of the population. This anticipated increase in demand for health care services is only one of a number of crises facing our current unwieldy and often ineffective health care system. Our study attempted to provide some answers to the question of how to meet the increased health care needs of the elderly without overwhelming the system.

This study used what is called the Delphi Method as a means of assessing experts' opinions about the current health-care system for the elderly. The Delphi technique sampled (repeatedly) the pool of expert professionals' wisdom about the good, the bad and the puzzles of elder health care. The participants were ninety-four health care professionals acknowledged as experts in gerontology through their work in research, practice, education or policy-making.

Measures

Round 1: An open-ended questionnaire, created for the study, was used in both the U.S. and U.K. versions. This open-end format was designed to minimize influence on the experts' responses and allow maximum latitude in answering. The following questions were used.

1. How well is the present health care system in the United States (United Kingdom) serving the needs of the elderly?
2. What are the main impediments to optimal health care delivery in the elderly?
3. What changes, if any, are needed to improve health care service to the elderly?
4. What is American (British) culture's underlying ideology regarding aging?
5. What responsibilities do health care professionals have to the elderly?
6. What responsibility, if any, does government have to the elderly?

7.   What kind of preparation is needed by health care profes-
      sionals working with or for elderly individuals in the fol-
      lowing areas: biomedical, psychosocial and existen-
      tial/spiritual?
8.   What are the essential skills and knowledge health care
      practitioners should acquire in order to deal effectively
      with the elderly?
9.   In your field, how are these skills and knowledge best ac-
      quired?
10.   In your estimation to what extent do health care profes-
      sionals working with or for the elderly in your field
      demonstrate these essential skills and knowledge?
11.   To what extent are your answers concerning the elderly
      based on the age of the individual and to what extent are
      they based on health condition?

Round 2: Responses from Questionnaire 1 formed the basis
for Questionnaire 2. Duplicate and overlapping items were combined to
produce a closed-ended checklist of the most frequently given responses.

Round 3: Statistical analysis of the findings, and a summary
of noteworthy quotations from the respondents, were prepared.

Discussion of Results

This study began with the assumption that identified experts in
aging would be able to articulate their opinions about the current state
of and the ideology shaping health care for the elderly in the United
States. It was further assumed that the experts would be able to provide
useful information about the impediments to optimal health care, the
changes necessary for improvement and the responsibilities of health
care professionals toward their elderly clients. The experts proved
themselves well able to do so.

Respondents showed a high rate of agreement about the health
care needs of their elderly clients and shared a common perception that
the present health care system is particularly inadequate in meeting the
needs of those elderly citizens who are least able to access necessary
services. Whether these elderly citizens lack the financial means to ac-
quire services or do not have the necessary know-how to connect with

services, in the opinions of the experts, these elders' health care needs are largely going unmet.

The experts expressed strong opinions about prohibitive costs and the need for a national health insurance. They demonstrated an admirable awareness of and sensitivity to their elderly clients' biopsychosocial needs in ways that often transcended their individual disciplines. Many of the professionals wrote eloquently about the need for continuity of care. The lack of preventive care was one of the most frequently made points of this study. Elderly citizens, perhaps more than any other group, are negatively affected by a lifetime's lack of preventive health care.

One value of this study lies in its clear demonstration of the degree to which health care practitioners involved in services to elderly clients share common perceptions about the needs of their clients. A high rate of agreement existed from the first round of the study, when experts were asked simply to state their opinions, and in the second round sampling. Identifying these shared perceptions makes it possible to shape policy and allocate monies with greater precision. The data from this study, and others that may follow, provide some indicators of boundaries and ways to organize needed changes in health care for the elderly.

This study shows that U.S. health care experts are bothered by the excessive focus on hospital care rather than a broader continuity of health care. If lack of preventive health care is, indeed, a major problem in the current system, what preventive measures are needed to help correct this problem?

A broader preventive emphasis in elder health care could also rectify many of the problems highlighted in this study. Lowered costs, increased awareness of psychosocial issues and a changed perspective of old age itself are but a few of the predictable changes that would follow from a national focus on preventive health care. These are precisely the areas for change identified by our respondents.

Health care reform has been a political issue for most of this century. Such programs as Social Security, Medicare, Medicaid and unemployment insurance have all addressed the continual crisis in health care without providing more than a temporary easing of the crisis. A social program with a scope necessary to truly reform American health care has never before been attempted.

Reform might take many possible directions. Creating a payment system that reimburses for treating the total patient rather than for isolated services and procedures would help to eliminate unnecessary medical procedures and curb "defensive medicine." It would also change the focus from treating health problems to preventing health problems. Moving away from physicians as the primary point of contact with the health care system by making use of allied professionals would cut costs and also dilute physicians' dominance in health care. Imposing caps on drug prices would curb the indefensible disparities in pricing. Aggressive public education campaigns on the need for both reform and prevention would help the American public first understand the issues, and second, pressure government to enact the necessary legislation. Adopting an employer-based or government-based approach rather than the current private market approach would encourage health care providers to compete for patient loyalty by offering caring, high-quality services rather than by price competition.

Action for reform, however, must be far more than governmental controls imposed on the present system. We need strong committed leadership at the national level to accomplish health care reform. Real reform must begin by defining its goal. That goal should be the improved health of American citizens, not simply improved reimbursement procedures, greater access to health care or cost controls. Elder Americans will benefit from health care reform to the extent that such reforms improve the health of all Americans.

The second part of our Delphi study of health care services for the elderly involved a parallel sample from Great Britain. This was titled:

HEALTH CARE NEEDS OF THE ELDERLY: A COMPARISON OF THE UNITED STATES AND UNITED KINGDOM USING THE DELPHI PROCESS (STUDY 2)

This study used the same format as the U.S. research, except that we sampled eighty-eight health care professionals in the United Kingdom, primarily in the middle to south of England. J. G. Evans, M.D. (Butler, 1992), professor of geriatric medicine at the University of Oxford, described the United Kingdom as having a socialized system of health and social services, making a comprehensive range of hospital, primary care and social facilities available to all elderly people.

During our Delphi study in Great Britain, their national health service was being significantly revamped. Four of the more than one dozen hospitals in London (where U.K. physicians are traditionally trained) were threatened with closing. There is a move toward "privatization" of the national system. In their instance, this meant moving some services into the private free market format, while still attempting to preserve the basics of a health care system that was accessible to all citizens. Many of the structures of patient referral (historically primary care physicians are the gatekeepers who decide when specialized consultations or procedures are needed) may also be modified. General practitioners in the English system still remain the "gatekeepers," but demarcation of which services fall under the health care division and which services fall under the social service division was a changing balance. When the senior author visited with practitioners in England, they would greet him with enthusiasm about finding out how U.S. competitive managed health care systems work. News that the U.S. versions often were not working well seemed to dampen their spirits. In sum, both the U.K. and U.S. health care systems were undergoing periods of change at the time of these parallel Delphi studies.

A review by Furnish (1994) considered the psychological and related medical needs of older people as recipients of health services in Great Britain. Well-developed data are lacking on the needs of older people and their families or care givers (as service users and potential users). Furnish argues effectively that even though strong relations between psychological factors and medical service utilization are well known, health service options often do not blend medical, psychological and social resources. The article provides a brief but thoughtful summary on major themes such as high morale versus depression, openness versus resistance to seeking services, benefits of treating caregivers as well as older patients, and benefit versus harm of "reminiscence" treatment techniques. The issues raised by Furnish are important as one considers the main structure of the United Kingdom's evolving system of care.

The U.K. system is structured basically in three parts (Liddiard and Ritvo, 1986). The first involves hospital-based services and a consistent network of regional health authorities. Interlocking, overlapping and sometimes complex sets of national district and local health authorities exist to govern or oversee health care functions. Not all hospital primary care services are managed with private practitioners on a capitalization payment system (meaning a pre-arranged payment for each type of service). The second part of the system is similar to the HMO (health maintenance organization) systems seen in the United States. HMOs are a fee-for-service system, with the general practitioner monitoring referrals for consultation and additional services. The third division of the British system involves personal social services. The review by Liddiard and Ritvo (1986) suggests that it would have been difficult to devise a system that had more possible problems inherent than Britain's. However, they also felt that it was remarkable how well this system could work when it was governed or managed locally (p. 307). Because the public sector of the health care system in Britain has been underfunded for many years, the government has encouraged the use of voluntary (not for profit and private) systems of care. Butler (1992, p. 40) also noted that strong ideological forces have caused a move in long-term nursing care from the national health service to the private sector or the social service and social security budget. In our conversations with people working in health care systems in Great Britain, we were impressed with the strong tradition and pride in a so-cialist system.

Whereas the word *socialism* often strikes terror in the hearts of red-blooded Americans, it is spoken with reverence and affection by many health providers we interviewed in England. The United Kingdom has taken pride in offering universal entitlement to services for its citizenship, and has expressed guilt in moving away from that system. The British professionals sampled were hopeful about finding a system with a better financial working, but fearful that their system's cherished universal access component could be lost.

The U.K. and U.S. health care systems were moving targets when we sampled professionals' opinions of their health services for older adults during 1992–1995. Some of the qualitative contrasts and similarities included the following. The U.K. professionals were less pessimistic about the quality of health care provided by their country than their counterparts in America. In the United States, a significant number of experts rated health care for the elderly as inadequate for those who do not have the financial resources or knowledge about how to gain access to the services. One U.K. respondent spoke for a number of colleagues by writing, "compared with many other countries our older people are being well served." However, many of the British professionals still thought much needed to be done to improve care (Gilleard, Askham, Biggs and Woods, 1995). In the United Kingdom, access to major services (basic care rather than specialists) seems easier to obtain than in the United States (Sachs, 1993). Sachs found that in both countries the health care plight was frightening for elderly with limited finances. The gatekeeper or service broker, as they are usually called in the United States, plays an important role in both countries in deciding what services will be paid for. If those gatekeepers and service brokers are involved in both the provision of health care *and* policy-making (in contrast to policies that are made by someone not involved in health care), they can make a positive difference in how well the system functions. The perception of many U.S. service providers is that the gatekeeper who works for a funding agency, either public or private, is interested first in cost containment and second in quality of patient care. In the United Kingdom, general practice physicians are used as the gatekeepers who allocate the services. It remains to be seen if service providers will have a similar perception of service brokers when those brokers are also engaged in direct patient care. Many respondents in the United States study felt that the further removed from the provision of health care the decision makers are, the more suspect are the ethics and quality of health care. Professionals from both countries agreed that ageism was a destructive force operating in health care. Overall, the health care provider's respect for his or her patients was considered to be the critical component in treatment.

The two parallel studies highlight more cautions than clear recommendations about what each country could learn from the other. The main strength in each country's health care system seemed to reside in the commitment of the individual professional rather than from any official policy.

One other factor worth emphasizing is the contrast between the U.S. and U.K. governments. Both countries have a participatory democracy system, even though Great Britain is still a monarchy by history. The ways policy decisions are made (and finances and budgets are compiled and spent) are qualitatively different in each country. This difference was described nicely by the late Prime Minister Harold Wilson in his 1976 book *The Governance of Britain*. In a chapter titled "Transatlantic Comparisons," Wilson said that in his final schooling at Oxford in 1937, one of his examination questions was, "Would you prefer to be the Prime Minister of the United Kingdom or President of the United States? State your reasons."

"Put simply, the President, elected directly and separately, is virtually secure from all possible removal. Nevertheless, part or even the whole of his tenure may be frustrated by an ability, or lack thereof, to get his legislation, including vital tax and financial legislation, through a hostile congress. The president cannot even expect success when he has a congress with a majority from his own party" (1976 p. 169). Wilson goes on to describe that the prime minister is in more danger because he can be thrown out of office on short notice if he loses control of Parliament. However, the British advantage for planning a health care system (and decisions about service inclusions and funding of the system) is that the prime minister can get most legislation carried through to the statute book without facing prickly modifications or the contentious atmosphere that earmarks U.S. legislation.

The United States has a peculiar method of creating legislative bills involving political compromise "riders." These riders have nothing to do with the core legislation itself. They create a truncated and adversarial path to lawmaking. The U.S. system often develops policies arising out of conflict rather than cooperation. It is our tenet that health care with a balance of body, mind and spirit is hard to create. Such a system is even harder to create in America when legislative policy is shaped by patchwork laws, lobbyists and special interests, and political parties more bent on diluting each other's powers than on creating an ethical health care system with sane policies for healthy mind, body and spirit. In Great Britain no member of the legislature, regardless of his party, can increase expenditure on a bill or policy near to his heart or constituency, and no member can "do a deal" with another member or group where they "scratch each other's backs." The significant fact of Westminster politics is that, as long as the government can win its battle in the division lobby (even by single-figure majorities in a house of over six hundred members), it can get its (budget and) business through. Nowhere is this more clear than in financial legislation, expenditure and taxation (Wilson, 1976, p. 169).

The British legislative system, then, may be better suited to devise and find cooperative policies in major health and social areas. Overall, the British system creates a more cooperative atmosphere to guide national health care policy than the American system. Unfortunately (relative to the United States), Britain has fewer financial resources to fund their plan. They are moving toward a privatization component of uncertain fit with their national health system.

AN INTEGRATED STORY, LESSONS FROM RESEARCH

In mental health and psychotherapy, interesting research has been done on the possibility of negative effects from treatment. Earlier we also discussed *iatrogenic* symptoms in medical care. These are problems or illnesses caused by the physician or the health care system. The conclusions from the research on harmful psychotherapy were varied, yet informative. The ways to avoid harmful treatment from therapy have been summarized nicely. The best guarantee against harmful effects is a professional who is informed and concerned. That principle is powerful in its simplicity. We know something about how to make sure that a health care provider is informed, and we can recognize those who are concerned. These are the qualities we want from professionals who treat us and our families. Training those qualities is the highest objective.

Health care must involve prevention, treatment and rehabilitation. When cost-containment is the only consideration, most spending will be for acute treatment; the need to "stop the bleeding." If acute treatment is the overvalued focus, then continuity of care for the older adult is likely to be compromised. The research reviewed suggested that 80 percent of the cost of health care for the older adult is spent in the last few months of life, treating the end stages of a terminal disease. Our understandable urgency in treating acute problems and attempting to cut costs can all but ignore the prevention and rehabilitation phases of health care. Psychological health and well-being can be relegated to an afterthought rather than create a force for prevention and resilience which enhances medical treatment. Similarly, ignoring the benefits of a spiritual dimension of life, or unnecessarily separating this dimension from health care, can keep us always chasing our tails—never doing more than "stopping the bleeding."

Much care for the elderly is considered palliative rather than curative. These adjectives evoked strong emotion in the experts we interviewed. Conservatively, research on medical expenditure and treatment given by primary care physicians shows that 50 percent of the problems for which people see a general practitioner have a primary psychological component. Health care policy must include wisdom and ethics in pre-vention, treatment and rehabilitation. If health providers are *not* the ones making decisions about allocation of health dollars, the policy-makers also must be informed and concerned about what comprises health and good health care. Where "case managers" or "quality assur-ance" overseers are not involved in treatment (but are financially re-warded for limiting treatment), they must share the liability risks for harm to patients.

The familiar dichotomy, still useful in contrasting health care systems, is the issue of whether health care is a right or a privilege. We doubt that the question is just that simple. The American system shows a duplicity in this issue because it is true that excellent health care is available, but perhaps only if one has enough money. Current political wars are struggling to find a more humane or a more practical answer. The United States seems to be moving toward uniform health care policy, if not uniform access. In contrast, Great Britain, while keeping some health care accessible to all, is moving in the direction of market competition and privatization. It appears then that the best guarantee against harmful health care includes both practitioners *and* policy-makers who are informed and concerned.

Recurrent emerging themes from the research on both sides of the Atlantic include the following issues organized under the headings of *Ills* and *Needs*.

Ills

- Most people want to live longer, but no one wants to grow old. There is a loss of personal meaning related to poorly defined roles of the aged in our culture.
- We have not clarified our decision on what is a right and what is a privi-lege in health care. As Callahan (1995) argues, we have not developed an ethical yet well-informed plan for allocating resources. The three cultures of medicine, religion and psychology too rarely work in con-cert to promote health and healing.
- The high-tech/biomedical treatment focus in aging is overvalued, to the relative exclusion of monies for prevention and recovery.
- Ageism in health care professionals has meant that *third agers* are not treated with the same vigor and totality of concern as are younger peo-ple.
- There is no dignity in either the need or receipt of services.

Needs

- An ethic must emerge for health and health care informed by all three cultures, body, mind and spirit, which guides a balanced model for delivery of services and allocation of resources. Prevention, treatment and recovery must be equally valued.
- The process of normal aging must be understood as well as the problems.
- We must celebrate lives and aging, not just honor people at their funerals. Part of this may include a greater acceptance of death in the context of life stages, generativity and multigenerational and cultural legacies.
- Conditions and problems are multideterminant rather than single-cause determinant. Therefore, multidimensional assessment models (to include physical, psychosocial and spiritual aspects) are sorely required. We must consider *functional age* more than *chronological age*. Problems and solutions in aging evolve from a web of causation.
- There is a joy in knowing and treating older adults. Appreciating aging as the realization of growth in the face of change is a renewing discovery. Humor, irony and perspective help preserve identity and dignity throughout life. If we can grasp this, we will honor both seniors and ourselves and begin to remove ageism.
- Training for caregivers, healers and health professionals must be creative and informed by these ills and needs.

The following thoughts were developed as answers to several of our major original questions. They integrate a realistic yet hopeful path to healthier health care for third agers.

1. *How well is the present health care system serving the needs of the elderly?*
    Most elderly live independently, are relatively healthy and receive good to excellent health care. Certain subpopulations of the elderly are less well served:
    a. The elderly poor, particularly those living in the inner city, and the rural poor.
    b. The homeless and mentally ill elderly.
    c   Ethnic Americans, especially those for whom English is a second language.
    d. The elderly suffering from long-standing, severe chronic illness, particularly illnesses derived from lifestyle choices (e.g., smoking, alcohol, high-calorie/high fat diets).

e.   The infirm, very aged elderly, persons over 85 whose needs are more custodial than health care. These five subcategories are poorly served; their care is fragmented, more designed to suit the convenience of the health care system and little concerned with those powerful socioeconomic issues. Those issues can deprive these elderly of the kind of qualitatively superior care available to middle-class elderly who are financially independent and mobile.

2.   *What are the main impediments to optimal health care delivery in the elderly?*
The impediments are, in a way, idiosyncratic to the above-named population subgroups:

a.   Geographic maldistribution; primary care physicians and supporting health care staff unavailable in their area.

b.   Lack of transportation to reach ambulatory health care facilities.

c.   Loss of the extended family linkages needed to sustain their independent "survival" in the presence of relatively minimal illness.

d.   System fragmentation, requiring multiple visits across differing specialties, laboratory and ancillary services.

e.   Unyielding addiction to alcohol, tobacco and high-caloric/high-fat diets.

f.   Relative disinterest by many health professionals in the elderly as people or in seeing their illness as not "worthy" of professional interest. (Poverty and a foreign language add exponentially to professional disinterest, if not repugnance, towards the elderly).

g.   Poverty; it simply takes money to follow through on adequate self-care from proper diet to the cost of medications through the taxi fare to the clinic.

h.   Isolation; living alone, like poverty, impedes one's ability to access health services or follow through on them once prescribed. Follow through on prescribed care often requires a caregiving relative or friend.

3.   *What changes, if any, are needed to improve health care service to the elderly?*

a.   Primary care physicians not specialists. The United States is a market-driven economy. Until we reverse the anomalous situation that pays surgeons on an hourly ba-

sis ten times what internists receive, there will not be
the needed movement toward care of the elderly by
physicians and other health professionals.

b. Programs effective in midlife (and before) which will reduce addiction to alcohol, tobacco and high-caloric diets,
themselves inevitably leading to much that we call illness in the elderly: hypertension, the alcohol-related
diseases, cardiac disease, much cancer, emphysema,
chronic obstructive pulmonary disease (COPD), plus
much loss of cognitive function and mobility consequent
to alcohol, drugs and obesity.

c. Systems of services that target their programs and are
organized structurally around the peculiar needs of the elderly. (HMOs typically eschew the elderly because their
costs of care are inordinately higher than the young, and
they are paid, per capita, for care of the relatively
healthy.) Thus, elderly care systems of service need to
be remunerated at the higher costs required in the care of
elderly individuals.

d. Redesign of our reimbursement structure, not only to
emphasize primary care but also to deemphasize the excessive costs of terminal care. This is a very complex
moral and ethical issue beyond the scope of this questionnaire. Nonetheless, a third to a half of one's lifetime
health care costs are expended in the last months of
one's lifetime (when one is not even likely to be conscious of the effort). These monies desperately need to
be expended on (a) prevention, (b) better ambulatory care
through the late middle years (forestalling the roots of
later illness), and (c) providing infrastructure and support
to the very old (before they become terminal and while
they are still capable of enjoying independence within
an assisted living environment).

e. Medical training which is essentially institutional training and glorifies the high-tech inpatient model. As
above, it overemphasizes the last days of the dying elderly, which tends to frighten and put off young trainees
and offers them little experience in or knowledge about
the healthy elderly and the kinds of programs needed to
service them.

4.   *What responsibility do health care professionals have to the elderly?*
      To take good care of their patients; to listen; to hear the elderly out in terms of their presentation of "symptoms" and yet to see their requests within a larger socioeconomic context that includes such issues as a sense of identity and self-esteem. Professionals should not define the aging process as itself pathologic.

      Conversely, health care professionals have a responsibility to treat real illness in the aged with vigor and with the same totality of concern with which they approach younger people with the same illness. By that we mean "bad" disease in the elderly—cancer of the breast, for example, dismissed without aggressive treatment merely because the individual is 90 years old. Unfortunately, the consequences of that dismissal lead to agonizing, terrible deaths dragged out over many months: of infection, of putrefaction that smells so bad no one will even enter the room to care for the dying.

      Lastly, health care professionals are small cogs in giant wheels. They cannot correct poverty, neighborhoods of crime, fragmented families or excessive alcoholism. It is *society* that created the system and bears final responsibility for the systems and institutions it creates and within which its health care professionals practice.

5.   *What responsibility, if any, does government have to the elderly?*
      a.   Decide if health care is to be a right or a privilege (for those who can afford it). If health care is to be a "right" for the elderly, as Medicare seems to imply, then government should adequately fund the nonreimbursable components for those individuals too poor to take care of the unpaid portions themselves.
      b.   Develop reimbursement mechanisms that reward primary care andsystems of services to the elderly, and that support noninstitutional care of the elderly within supported housing, assisted living and fostercare living arrangements.
      c.   Develop reimbursement mechanisms in support of the housing and companionship needs of the very aged who are not themselves sick but are unable to live independently (or unable to access the current health system on their own).

d. Help eliminate smoking. Smoking remains the largest single remediable cause of illness and premature death in the elderly.

e. Help reduce alcoholism.

f. Work to eliminate the unconscionable costs of administration in the delivery of health care services. Currently, 25 percent or more of all our health insurance dollars goes to support the administrative costs of the insurance operations. A move to a single "insurer," simplified reimbursement mechanisms and the elimination of paper work could pay the entire costs of health care for the 30 million presently uninsured.

6. *What kind of preparation is needed by health care professionals working with or for elderly individuals in the following areas?*

a. *Biomedical*—greater acquaintance with the healthy aged living independent and productive lives; greater time spent learning and practicing in ambulatory and home health care-type facilities so as to have a sense of the natural history of illness as it truly occurs for the majority of elderly; and lastly, to be part of teaching institutions that themselves are professionally and financially rewarded for maintaining individuals out of nursing homes and chronic institutions.

b. *Psychosocial*—again greater familiarity with the healthy aged to both understand both the process of aging and the enormous life contributions of the individual elderly, something gained only through time spent working with them. Faculties should help students in the psychosocial arena come to terms with their own feelings about and fears of the aging process itself, exploring with them the ageist media "brainwashing" that created our culture of youth.

c. *Existential/spiritual*—help Americans reexamine their own belief system in the meaning and purpose of life.

As previously mentioned, there needs to be an agonizing reappraisal of the provision of health care services to the terminally aged. For example, home health and ambulatory services that could keep people *out* of the nursing homes should have a higher priority than institutions.

7.   *What essential skill and knowledge should health care practition-*
     ers acquire in order to deal effectively with the elderly?
     Lots of time needs to be spent with the elderly in order to learn
     about them as real people. This best starts with the healthy, suc-
     cessful aged, individuals who, for example, have raised families in
     the inner city, who are still caring for their grandchildren's ba-
     bies, who are pillars of their church, who are still holding down
     part time jobs. Then they need to learn the skills of how to car-
     ingly "manipulate" the families and social system of the elderly in
     order to improve their clients' health situations. Helping to bring
     a daughter or son-in-law into the aged patient's health crisis may
     be as important as any medicine. Lastly, young practitioners
     should learn that while aging cannot be "cured," maintaining an
     elderly individual independently in his or her own home, albeit
     temporary, is an achievement of the highest caliber. Equally, to
     comfort the aged, to nurture their passage through their final years
     is a medical challenge of great complexity. The system needs to
     reward its teachers for conveying this posture to its students.

8.   *In your estimation, to what extent do health care professionals*
     working with or for the elderly in your field demonstrate these es-
     sential skills and knowledge?
     Variable. The nursing profession is often highly skilled in this
     area, and whole nursing agencies, such as home health care, are a
     veritable storehouse of skills and wisdom in dealing with the el-
     derly. In every profession there are good, dedicated people who
     offer informed and inspired care. They should be better identified
     and held up as models.

There are difficult but necessary choices to be made. Callahan
(1995) has urged that setting limits should be considered and accomplished with an informed and a concerned, yet realistic, design. When
shaping health care (its scope, its focus, its funding and its ethics), financial savings alone must not guide the effort. In our attempts to
shape health care too often a thoughtful grand design is nowhere to be
found. A wish that all clinical services and procedures be available for
everyone is naive. Too often policies that drive health care delivery
systems have been trimmed and chopped by budget crises and ad hoc interests. However, an ethical model for good health care can emerge if
advised by the reality of multiple causation and the multiple needs of
body, mind and spirit.

Not only will scientists have to grapple with the sciences that deal with people, but—and this is a far more difficult matter—they will have to persuade the world to listen to what they have discovered. If he cannot succeed in this difficult enterprise, man will destroy himself with his halfway cleverness.

—Bertrand Russell

NOTES

Carol Ballard, Psy.D. is Director of the Counseling Center at Florida Southern College, Lakeland, Florida.

Jeff S. Rain, Ph.D. is Consulting Psychologist at Rain & Brehm Consulting Team, Rockledge, Florida.

Karl Sachs, Psy.D. is a Psychologist at Arizona Children's Home, Tucson, Arizona.

Robert M. Vidaver, M.D. is Professor and Vice Chair of the Department of Psychiatry at Dartmouth Medical School, Hanover, New Hampshire and Medical Director at New Hampshire Hospital, Concord, New Hampshire.

8

Implications for Health
Professionals

Themes and strategies outlined throughout the book can help health professionals, policy-makers and caregivers promote a balanced story of health care for older adults. If the interactions of body, mind and spirit are ignored, then health care is not healthy. Medicine, psychology and spirituality are powerful, but each can also be harmful if they neglect the other dimensions of health. In this final chapter we wish to ensure that health professionals are *aware* of the essential dimensions of healing, and that they are *concerned* enough to apply a healthy balance of soma, psyche and spirit. Also, we suggest some new ways for society, professionals and mature adults to view this special time of life.

The first part of the chapter restates guiding principles for health professionals who work with older adults, and the second part considers some therapy applications. Psychotherapy is the treatment arena considered. However, these principles also apply to medical and spiritual domains. Storytending is a helpful metaphor for therapy and healing, and it is also a valuable strategy to keep our profession and craft healthy.

A humane ethic for care will draw on rigorous medical knowledge and practice buoyed by scientific advances. Yet these strengths must be balanced by a caring appreciation for our limitations and dependence on natural healing forces guided by psychological and spiritual principles as well.

As stated earlier, there are two distinct yet intertwined themes in this book: healthy aging and healthy treatment. The first theme is that the healthiest people in life's third age have been able to preserve an enduring sense of identity in their life story. Balancing change and continuity across the stages of life is rarely an easy task. Fortunately resilience and perspective are often a treasured result of overcoming life's challenges. The second theme suggests ways to heal health care, and to make a wiser tale. This plot blends medical, psychological and spiritual dimensions of healing characterized by wisdom, skill and concern, while devoid of ageism. The business of medicine must struggle with the tension between seemingly unlimited scientific and technological advances balanced against the harsh reality of limited fiscal resources. The hard questions are, who sets the limits and how are those resources allocated?

A third theme, the *minimal interference principle*, can help balance tensions between the other two themes. This strategy offers an elegant unifying simplicity. Minimal interference means aggressive, humane and decisive treatment, but no more than necessary. Such parsimony helps keep costs to a minimum. A least obtrusive strategy honors people's sense of worth, their life struggles and triumphs, while building upon personal and family strengths developed across the lifespan. Applications of the principle have been suggested throughout the book.

Healthy aging is a theme woven through a lifetime and even across generations. *Third agers* can preserve meaning and purpose through a life story reconsidered and revised as needed. This story repair may come in response to joy, challenge, loss and growth. The story of health care also periodically needs a rewrite. The antidote for noxious elder health care includes professional caregivers who:

> are aware and concerned
> demonstrate integrity, knowledge and commitment
> make ethical and informed decisions about resource allocation

Who can best help revise life stories gone awry? Friends or family members may become the healing listener. Often, however, a psychotherapist's skills are needed, not only to listen but also to create or reclaim a resilient sense of self and hope. Whose job is it to reform an ill health care system? Perhaps everyone is needed to create a unified vigilance. Concerned advocates can include patients, families, senior watchdog groups, legislators and caregivers from medical, psychological and spiritual cultures. All may be needed to heal and reform health care.

PRINCIPLES FOR PSYCHOTHERAPISTS

Good treatment for seniors demands an appreciation of informed principles. People need an enduring identity and a sense of self in spite of life's surprises from losses, stress and change. A therapist must appreciate the evolution of seasons, themes and dreams. Physical, psychological and spiritual dimensions must be understood in balance.

Life's last stage involves a trip inventory of sorts. This life review process (whether conscious or implicit) ponders one's life journey. Do we come closer to a sense of integrity or to a sense of despair? Understanding how we faced the challenges of identity, intimacy, generativity and integrity (along with a sense of humor) may give us a sextant with which we set our course.

Therapy with older adults and their families is rewarding yet humbling. Techniques for therapy are important, but equally important are principles that engender hope. Together, strategies and hope are the core of healing. Crucial qualities unique to effective psychotherapy with older patients were described in more detail in chapter one. Those qualities include: (1) a thoughtful appreciation of human development and the life cycle of both individuals and families, (2) an understanding of the impact of losses and how to use change to grow and heal, (3) an appreciation for the difference between normal and pathological aging with a knowledge of how physical and psychological aspects interact, and (4) the ability to honor, clarify and preserve a person's complex sense of self, balancing people's need for continuity and change. Health professionals who incorporate these qualities honor the people we treat.

A THERAPY STORY

Diverse health professionals (e.g. Akeret, 1991;   Carlsen, 1991; Dossey, 1993; Gutmann, 1987; Haley, 1976; Hudson & O'Hanlon, 1991; Kaufman, 1986; Stoddard, 1992; Vash, 1994; Viney, 1993; Stoddard, 1992) are creating new and rediscovering old ways to reclaim strengths and resources which draw on all three cultures of healing. The process goes by different names like cure, healing, learned optimism, or respiriting. Widening the vision of medical practice based on scientific knowledge alone benefits everyone involved. It is possible to clarify and preserve a person's complex identity across the lifespan. A psychotherapist does this directly with older adults and their families (or sometimes involves their friends) by helping them discover, tell and modify their life stories to a state of meaning, satisfaction or acceptance.

The most effective psychotherapists are gifted at discovering, honoring and healing patients' personal stories. There is an acquirable skill that discerns the core dynamic, leit motif, life themes or hopes and fears that propel us. These life themes are the fabric of identity and meaning. When these stories need tending or changing, we must recall the minimal interference principle and honor the person by making the least change necessary while preserving the core of a person's identity. Not surprisingly, a health care designed to value personal worth and continuity of care, across the medical, psychological and spiritual domains, is the best landscape for emotional and physical health.

A therapy story about a senior couple, Bob and Helen, may help clarify the process of forming and reforming each of their identities, as well as revising the story of their relationship together.

Bob and Helen have been married for more than twenty-five years. Together they have an adult son, daughter-in-law and grandchild. Bob was referred to the treating psychologist by his neurologist. Bob came with symptoms of agitated depression, a strong conviction that he needed a divorce in order to get relief from various frustrations and an unnamed anger that was currently haunting him. The referral from the physician also asked to consider whether there was a dementing neurological disease. Bob was an interesting, proud and intelligent man. At the same time he was opinionated but possessed a redeeming sense of humor. He usually could get a new perspective on himself in response to firm confrontation. Bob had a number of successes in his adult life. He was a military officer in the second world war. He carried a strong part of his identity in the traditional pride and rigors of standing up for what he believed in. After his retirement from the military, he was able to make the transition into civilian life as an engineer involved in the NASA space program. Now in retirement he and his wife are financially stable and comfortable, but he still had his engine running high to create and offer his opinion in a number of areas. At times he shared with the therapist articles he had written on topics from revamping the IRS to a touching and insightful look at his experience of prostate cancer and surgery.

Bob had been married before. There was little contact from his ex-wife, but his sons who lived three hours away were a low-level stressor or anxiety for him. He often second guessed himself on how he raised the boys and what he might be able to do now to redirect them.

Several years ago he was hospitalized for depression and significant mood swings. He said his previous psychological treatment was most beneficial and he talked with high regard for the psychiatrist who had managed his medication and therapy.

Bob related, in bits and pieces, the story of his years growing up. He was raised by a demanding and emotionally withholding mother (in his view). He felt that she never gave him the praise or affirmation that he dearly sought. He vacillated between being angry at the mother who raised him and the father who was not around to do so. In Bob's recollection, he learned not to dwell on the sadness, but rather made it the "strongest motivator of my life." He was prone to sharing stories of his struggles and successes in the Marines where he learned that challenge, determination and commitment to beliefs were the secrets to a successful life. He liked a good fight and never missed an opportunity to challenge the therapist and laugh uproariously when the therapist came back forcefully. He was comfortable with a confrontational approach, which allowed the therapist to point out how Bob contributed to marital conflicts. He said he liked it when the therapist called him a "horse's ass" when he was one.

Through neuropsychological testing we were able to rule out a dementing process. That is, his difficulties in memory and cognition were more related to his agitated depression. The consulting neurologist prescribed antidepressant medication which helped greatly. The therapy relationship was solidly created, and before too long Bob was receptive to bringing in his wife Helen.

Helen was a delightful woman twelve years younger. They had been married for more than a quarter of a century and as mentioned above had an adult son living not too far away from them. Helen was a recently retired teacher and an educational administrator in the last part of her formal working years. By listening to Bob's boasting and accompanying complaining about Helen's career, the therapist discovered that Helen was highly regarded as an ideal educator. She was the proto-type of an inspiring teacher. Families (across two generations) would return to visit and share with her the influence she had on their lives.

Helen was afraid Bob would present a slanted perspective on their marriage and his condition. She had developed some ways to con-tend with his forceful bravado and the other subtleties that motivated him. In retirement, he no longer had officer's rank or an engineer's status. Clearly she cared deeply for him, but Helen had her own recent medical difficulties. These included breast and ovarian cancer. Her can-cer had been in remission for over three years, but the anguish of a pos-sible return was never completely removed. In some ways Helen saw Bob's current angry depressed state as possibly a reoccurrence of the se-rious depression that hospitalized him years before. Helen was unsure whether to view his current condition with sympathy (since it followed on the heels of his operation for prostate cancer) or with protective anger that his maladies were simply selfish and petty.

Helen was the youngest of four daughters raised in a tradition-ally southern family. Her family was religious and she found some strength in her family, but also expressed resentment at never being able to rise above her status as the baby sister. Helen was a voracious reader and a good thinker. She helped the therapist and herself understand her role in her family and how some of those strivings translated into her marriage as well as her relation with Bob.

Helen had a circle of caring and supportive women friends. She often talked about how, without their support, she probably would have sent Bob packing in recent years. Bob frequently criticized Helen by rehashing how she allowed the school system to take advantage of her (she wasn't tough enough) in the past. He told her now to stand on her own and not be so inefficient and overfocused in relationships with her friends. He was jealous. Bob's repeated solution to situations was to get tougher. Helen was frustrated with her conflicting needs to nur-ture and be sympathetic to him, against the need to be defended lest he steamroll her. Usually, the subtlety eluded him, so the therapist often adopted a confronting and salty style of interacting with him. He liked a good fight. Unfortunately, that sometimes seemed to be his idea of in-timacy.

As the counseling progressed (interspersing individual sessions with couples counseling) we were able to clarify the leitmoifs, core fears and hopes and the hunches that propelled each of them. Together we were able to recognize each of their styles for trying to get their needs met, and the ways their stories collided. Through some irony and humor, we were able to caricature their defensive styles and fears, while at the same time validate their needs as healthy and meetable.

We also reflected on the serious cancer-related illnesses they were both surviving. In spite of their intermittent conflict, there was a history of supporting and caring for each other during these serious illnesses. They could protect one another, and they told stories of the cancer support groups (formal and informal) that had helped them through the toughest times. Part of their healing stories included shared anger at health professionals who had been insensitive, obstructive or even iatrogenic during the diagnostic, treatment or recovery phases. They were able to translate their shared anger and sadness into helpful suggestions about how the process could be rehumanized. Helen drew on her traditonal religious values and beliefs for strength. In contrast, Bob's spirituality is best characterized as a kind of "rage at the moon" agnosticism, which was tempered by his testimonial to the exceptional experience and benefit he derived from his cancer support group. In different ways they each had a spiritual style that helped the healing process. They also used the treating clinical/medical psychologist to communicate with their physicians, thereby helping coordinate aspects of their health care which otherwise lacked an integrated continuity of care. It seemed ironic that they were able to care for each other most effectively in the physical arena where life and death stakes are the highest.

Like most couples who have known each other for a long time, they were skilled at naming their partner's irritating ways of relating. Each of them could describe and label provocative (if not sinister) motives that the other might have for "not fighting fairly." At times each of them would be extremely defensive and unwilling to compromise or make concessions to the other. This is a common protective stance people take in marital conflict. However, we were able to clarify an important principle. The principle is that intimacy in a healthy relationship is a balance of the needs for control in the relationship (being an equal partner exerting an appropriately assertive influence), against the need for vulnerability (receiving caring and closeness in a safe emotional climate). After one of Bob's tirades Helen protectively moved back into her shell, and we took time to clarify the pattern. Helen reported that each time there was one of these explosions, Bob would come around and be apologetic. However, she was too vulnerable and defensive to trust his sincerity. Out of his own sense of vulnerability he was oblivious to the way his anger made her more defensive. A valuable funny quote was useful in clarifying this pattern to them: "The lion and the lamb will lie down together and the lamb won't get much sleep." On several occasions repeating this observation was enough for the two of them to laugh and defuse the tension. The image of that quote created a springboard to change the climate of the relationship; to make vulnerability safe, and control or influence shared. When that climate of safety or good faith is absent, protective strategies or symptoms develop instinctively. Balancing the paradoxical needs for control and vulnerability spawns intimacy. This is especially true when there is an enduring commitment to the relationship. A sense of humor also helps the prognosis.

Another metaphor that they warmed to is the notion of "getting your back scratched." This is a simple, straightforward and useful metaphor. I asked them what they would need to do to get their back scratched? This analogy for the process can be used without a lot of memory baggage that triggers certain hurts and fights in a couple's history.

The backscratching metaphor allows people to consider what communication steps are needed to clearly express one's needs, wishes and preferences, thereby sustaining communication in a way that encourages (rather than criticizes) each person to ask for help. Too often talking has broken down to the point where the only communication is to tell the other person how bad he or she is at sensing and meeting your needs. The analogy helps defuse blaming by rethinking the process and clarifying steps to get one's needs met. The metaphor also clarifies how each person's defensive strategy can almost guarantee that no one gets their itches nicely scratched. The metaphor also has a sexual undercurrent which can remain subtle at a time in therapy when explicitly addressing the sexual theme will only heighten fear, anger and conflict. Bob and Helen liked the process so well that they eventually brought the therapist a wooden backscratcher as a symbol of their appreciation and the rediscovery of their mutual caring and shared sense of humor.

Besides being an interesting couple, Bob and Helen are a good example of the way physical, psychological and spiritual issues may interact to help or hinder healthy aging. A health care system that minimizes mind/body overlap and looks only at physical problems, without psychological or spiritual resources, will only worsen the psychological wounds of medical problems each of them struggled with, at times "too much alone." If their isolation and evolved distrust of each other were not addressed, the sequelae of their physical illness could have been more bleak. In contrast, the rediscovery of their strong relationship bond from earlier times helped them "expect well," once again and revitalize their relation and their resilience. This process, as Helen noted, "is a garden that will always need tending."

This short story of a couple's treatment incorporates the central qualities we have stressed. There is an appreciation of the individual and family developmental landscapes and how they blend or collide. The therapist conveyed a sensitivity to their losses and their history of change. Then a conflictual pattern was described with humor to defuse fear and anger. This was followed by developing a strategy to regain support from each other. This was done by showing how each person's conflicting needs for control and vulnerability was keeping them apart. We were able to reclaim their intimacy; their ability to scratch each other's back. They were complex in the task of understanding the difference between normal and pathological aging, but getting to know them honored their strengths and made it safe for them to risk showing their perceived failures. Their health issues profoundly affected and impressed the therapist by the strength they both showed in facing cancer. In some measure we were able to strike a balance between their needs for change with their needs for continuity. We helped clarify and preserve the best qualities or their sense of self and the relationship. Rewriting a love story involves both individual and couple story editing. Finally, we had some success applying the minimal interference principle; changing only what needed changing while honoring past strengths. Physical, psychological and spiritual dimensions were all considered.

STORY TENDING

As mentioned before, the process of tending stories should involve not only the healing and growth of our patients, but also the health of our profession, science, art and craft. An important part of that process is knowing our strengths and our limitations. As professionals we also should heed Helen's advice. We too have "a garden that will always need tending."

In Chapter six, the concept of *triage* was explained as a metaphor for managing massive numbers of casualties in the face of limited resources. The writer James Michener (1996) in his book *This Noble Land* describes his own and his wife's experience with five bouts of cancer as well as his heart attack and quintuple bypass surgery. He notes that his experience was excellent, but he attributes that to his financial security. He noted that he had the unusual opportunity to see a confidential report on how best to use a healthy kidney that an automobile accident had supplied. The report asked, "Which of our patients can profit from this kidney?" Next to his name were the notes "Too old. Too many other medical problems." He agreed that in his case this was probably the right decision. However, he suggests that many of today's triage decisions in allocating limited resources are not based on the decisions of patients or informed health professionals, but on much more subtle factors such as ageism, greed or cost-containment without regard to larger issues. America's health care is in "a time of triage," and the principles for allocation of resources being made on this new battlefield are neither well articulated nor well applied.

Health professionals cannot escape the tension from pressures to reduce health costs and the need to preserve informed yet humane treatment. Such informed health care could be a healing blend of the best contributions that body, mind and spirit have to offer. All three cultures, medicine, psychology and religion, are vitally needed in a balanced way for life's third age; the senior years. Unfortunately, the cultures of medicine, psychology and religion may do more to further their own guild than to honor the contributions of all three parts. If health care focuses exclusively on acute medical treatment to cut costs, to the exclusion of prevention and recovery, then the psychological and spiritual dimensions of healing are left out of the equation. Without clear mind and renewed spirit, no amount of money or technology will produce an ethical way to treat people and preserve their personal stories and their personal legacies. Art, science, religion and psychology share a goal: to say or do a thing more clearly and honestly than it's been said or done before. The result advances health, knowledge, freedom and joy.

Medical, psychological and spiritual professionals must integrate the best principles of treatment, healing and renewal available to care for others. What knowledge and resources are undervalued and underused? Which creative strategies that have worked in the past are we forgetting or neglecting now? What wounds from the past have been untreated or overlooked? Too rarely have older adults been accurately portrayed or understood. We can breathe new life into the tale of maturing and the ways we promote and use the strengths and knowledge of older adults. Subplots for this new story could include the following.

1. Refocus health care with a wider lens on multidetermined health processes, not just biologically determined illness. Minimize the traditional acute medical care (hospital) system. Hospitals do not promote the best care for seniors. Models of community-based clinics with multidisciplinary professionals are available (Nussbaum, 1996). These settings offer continuity of care for both chronic and acute conditions. We can clarify the unique capabilities and resources seniors have in the areas of acquired wisdom, ability to thrive, robustness and learned optimism. Multiple needs, multiple knowledge and multiple abilities call for health care broadly conceived to include social, spiritual, physiologic and psychological in addition to medical resources. Managed health care can contain costs. However, without the cardinal value of continuity of care, health care can be iatrogenic. We ought to create a health care in which we would like to be treated.

2. Reframe and retell the story to reflect the realities and opportunities of maturing. Beginning early in school, community and religious settings, the hopeful facts of aging should be presented rather than ageist myths that have emphasized the negative. Similarly the media and advertising can help reflect hope, humor and anticipation rather than fear and pessimism. Business and education can lead the way in sponsoring and creating nontraditional avenues for seniors to express their talents and to forge new roles in mentoring, advising and policy-making. As baby boomers move into the third age their demands will be as vocal as they have been in all the earlier life stages of their generation. We need not wait for the boomers to make the changes seniors need now.

3. Consider ways that churches, temples and religious communities can create powerful and viable models of cross-generational interaction. This blending of the ages, if well-conceived, will be a nurturing, challenging and generative way to include and complement the life stages. Stage-of-life demands can be reframed and eased

by creating settings where the different generations interact with regard and caring. We can harness complementary needs and resources in multi-aged settings based
on inclusion and enduring values. The potential of such
communities to enrich future generations and combat the
isolation and ageism of today's seniors could awaken a
friendly slumbering giant.

Health professionals must expand their roles to become students of and advocates for creative solutions. How can we foster a true
continuity of care comprised of prevention, treatment and readjustment?
The spectrum of care must honor seniors' families as essential caregivers, because they must answer the question, "What will happen to us
when the experts are gone?" The conundrum to be solved is, how do we
balance ethical, caring and scientifically informed treatment with limited
resources? Voices of wisdom come from different cultures of care and
knowledge. Wisdom also comes from listening to our patients and
their families who do the enduring job of caregiving. Healthy aging and
healthy treatment emerge when professionals from all disciplines truly
value and integrate the best of soma, psyche and soul.

References

Akeret, R. U. (1991). *Family tales, family wisdom; How to gather the stories of a lifetime.* New York: William Morrow.

Aleichem, S. (1987). *Tevye the dairy man and the railroad stories* translated by Hillel Halkin. New York: Schocken Books.

Alexander, C. and Langer, E. (1990). *The higher stages of human development.* Oxford: Oxford University Press.

American Association of Retired Persons. (1990). *A profile of older Americans: 1990.* Washington, D.C.

Anderson, R. S. (ed.) (1975). *Pet animals and society.* London: Bailliere Tindall.

Atchley, R. C. (1989). A continuity theory of normal aging. *The Gerontologist, 29,* 183–190.

Baltes, P. B. (1997). On the incomplete architecture of human ontogeny: Selection, optimization, and compensation as foundation of developmental theory. *American Psychologist, 52,* 366–380.

Baltes, P. B. and Baltes, M. M. (1990). *Successful aging: Perspectives from the behavioral sciences.* Cambridge: Cambridge University Press.

Becker, G. and Kaufman, S. (1988). Old age, rehabilitation and research: A review of the issues. *The Gerontologist, 28,* 459–468.

Bengeston, V. L. and Treas, J. (1980). *The changing family context of mental health and aging.* Englewood Cliff, N.J.: Prentice-Hall.

Benson, H. (1996). *Timeless healing: The power and biology of belief.* New York: Scribner.

Benson, H. (1987). *Your maximum mind*. New York: Times Books/Random House.

Benson, H. (1984). *Beyond the relaxation response: How to harness the healing power of your personal beliefs*. New York: Times Books/Random House.

Benson, H. (1979). *The mind/body effect*. New York: Berkley Books.

Benson, H. (1975). *The relaxation response*. New York: William Morrow.

Berman, P. (1989). *The courage to grow old*. New York: Ballantine.

Bettelheim, B. (1976). *The uses of enchantment*. New York: Vintage.

Birren, J. E. and Deutchman, D. E. (1991). *Guiding autobiography groups for older adults: Exploring the fabric of life*. Baltimore: Johns Hopkins University Press.

Birren, J. E., Kenyon, G. M., Ruth, J.-E., Schroots, J. F. and Svensson, T. (1996). *Aging and biography: Explorations in adult development*. New York: Springer.

Birren, J. E. and Renner, V. J. (1981). Concepts and criteria of mental health and aging. *American Journal of Orthopsychiatry, 51,* 242–253.

Birren, J. E. and Schaie, K. W. (1985). *Handbook of psychology and aging*. New York: Van Nostrand.

Blazer, D. (1991). Spirituality and aging well. *Generations, 15,* 61–65.

Blazer, D. (1990). *Emotional problems in later life: Intervention strategies for professional caregivers*. New York: Springer.

Booth, W. (1992). *The art of growing older: Writers on living and aging*. New York: Poseidon Press.

Booth, W. C. (1992). Criticism and the pursuit of character. *Journal of Medical Humanities, 13,* 67–78.

Borysenko, J. (1988). *Minding the body, mending the mind*. New York: Bantam.

Boyle, N. (1992). Managed care as seen by a patient. *Psychiatric News*. September 18, 1992.

Bracero, W. (1996). The story hour: Narrative and multicultural perspective on managed care and time-limited psychotherapy. *Psychotherapy Bulletin* (APA Division 29), *31,* 59–65.

Brink, T. L. (1986). *Clinical gerontology: A guide to assessment and intervention*. New York: Haworth.

Brinton, H. (1964). *Friends for 300 years*. Wallingford, Pa.: Pendle Hill Publications.

Buber, M. (1995). *Martin Buber's ten rungs: Collected Hasidic sayings*. New York: Citadel Press.

Buber, M. (1958). *I and Thou* (second edition). New York: Scribner.

Butler, R. N. (1992). Geriatric primary care: A European perspective, part I. *Geriatrics, 47* (1), 31–41.

Callahan, D. (1995). *Setting limits: Medical goals in an aging society.* Washington, D.C.: Georgetown University Press.

Callahan, D. (1990). *What kind of life? The limits of medical progress.* New York: Simon and Schuster.

Campbell, J. (with Bill Moyers). (1988). *The power of myth.* New York: Doubleday.

Carlsen, M. B. (1991). *Creative aging: A meaning making perspective.* New York: W. W. Norton.

Carter, E. and McGoldrick, M. (eds.) (1989). *The changing family life cycle.* New York: Gardner Press.

Chinen, A. B. (1989). *In the everafter: Fairy tales for the second half of life.* Wilmette, Ill.: Chiron Publishers.

Cohen, D. and Eisdorfer, C. (1993). *Seven steps to effective parent care.* New York: Putnam.

Cohen, D. and Eisdorfer, C. (1986). *The loss of self: A family resource for Alzheimer's disease.* New York: Penguin.

Cohen, G. D. (1988). *The brain in human aging.* New York: Springer.

Coles, R. (1993). *Flannery O'Connor's south.* Athens: University of Georgia Press.

Coles, R. (1990). *The spiritual life of children.* New York: Houghton Mifflin.

Coles, R. (1989). *The call of stories: Teaching and the moral imagination.* Boston: Houghton Mifflin.

Cooper, W. (1990). *A living faith: An historical study of Quaker beliefs.* Richmond, Ind.: Friends United Press.

Corson, S. A. and Corson, E. O. (1982). Pet animals as socializing catalysts in geriatrics: An experiment in nonverbal communication therapy. In Lennart, L. (ed.) *Anxiety, stress and disease, Vol. 5.* Oxford: Oxford University Press.

Cousins, N. (1990). *Head first.* New York: Penguin.

Cox, M. and Theilgaard, A. (1987) *Mutative metaphors in psychotherapy.* London: Tavistock.

Dan, B. D. and Young, R. K. (1988). *A piece of my mind: A collection of essays from the Journal of the American Medical Association.* New York: Ballantine.

Davis, D. (1993). *Telling your own stories.* Little Rock, Ark.: August House.

DiGiovanna, D. (1994). *Human aging: Biological persectives.* New York: McGraw-Hill.

Dossey, L. (1993) *Healing words: The power of prayer and the practice of medicine.* New York: HarperCollins.

Dossey, L. (1989). *Recovering the soul: A scientific and spiritual search.* New York: Bantam.

Dychtwald, K. and Flower, J. (1989). *The age wave: Challenges and opportunities of an aging America.* Los Angeles: Tarcher, Inc.

Eisdorfer, C., Kessler, D. and Spector, A. N. (1989). *Caring for the elderly: Reshaping health policy.* Baltimore: Johns Hopkins University Press.

Epston, D. and White, M. (1989). *Literate means to therapeutic ends.* Adelaide, Australia: Dulwich Center Publishers.

Erikson, E. (1982). *The life cycle completed.* New York: W. W. Norton.

Erikson, E. (1980). *Identity and the life cycle.* New York: W. W. Norton.

Erikson, E. (1969). *Ghandi's truth.* New York: W. W. Norton

Erikson, E. (1964). *Insight and responsibility.* New York: W. W. Norton.

Erikson, E. (1958). *Young man Luther.* New York: W. W. Norton.

Estes, C. L. and Binney, E. A. (1989). The biomedicalization of aging: Dangers and dilemmas. *The Gerontologist, 29,* 587–596.

Fischer, K. (1985). *Winter grace.* New York: Paulist Press.

Fogle, B. (1981). *The human-companion animal bond.* Springfield, Ill.: Chas C. Thomas.

Fowler, J. W. (1981). *Stages of faith.* San Francisco: Harper and Row.

Framo, I. L. (1992). *Family of origin therapy: An intergenerational approach.* New York: Brunner/Mazel.

Frank, J. D. and Frank, J. B. (1991). *Persuasion and healing: A comparative study of psychotherapy.* Baltimore: Johns Hopkins University Press.

Frankl, V. (1973). *The doctor and the soul.* New York: Vintage.

Friedan, B. (1993). *The fountain of age.* New York: Simon and Schuster.

Friedman, E., Katacher, A. H., Lynch, J. J. and Thomas, S. A. (1980). Animal companions and one-year survival of patients after discharge from a coronary care unit. *Public Health Reports, 95,* 307–312.

Furnish, S. (1994). The psychological needs of older people as recipients of health services. *Clinical Psychology Forum* (British Psychological Society), *71,* 2–8.

Gatz, M. and Smyer, M. A. (1992). The mental health system and older adults. *American Psychologist, 47,* 741–751.

Gilleard, C., Askham, J., Biggs, H.B., Gibson, S. and Woods, B. (1995). Psychology, ageism and healthcare: A DCP symposium. *Clinical Psychology Forum* (British Psychological Society), *85,* 14–16.

Gilligan, C. (1983). *In a different voice: Psychological theory and women's development.* Cambridge, Mass.: Harvard University Press.

Gutmann, D. L. (1987). *Reclaimed powers: Towards a new psychology of men and women in later life. New York: Basic Books.*

Haley, J. (1976). *Problem-solving therapy: New strategies for effective family therapy.* New York: Jossey-Bass.

Hall, E. G. (1985). Spirituality during aging. *Pastoral Psychology, 34,* 112–117.

Hollstein, M. B. and Coles, T. R. (1996). Reflections on age, meaning and chronic illness. *Journal of Narrative and Life History.* Hillside, N.J.: Lawrence, Erlbaum and Associates Publisher.

Holmes, T. H. and Rahe, T. H. (1967). The social readjustment rating scale. *Journal of Psychosomatic Research, 11,* 213.

Homer, P. and Holstein, M. (1990). *A good old age: The paradox of setting limits.* New York: Simon and Schuster.

Howard, G. S. (1991). Culture tales: A narrative approach to thinking, cross-cultural psychology, and psychotherapy. *American Psychologist, 46,* 187–197.

Hudson, P. O. and O'Hanlon, W. H. (1991). *Rewriting love stories: Brief marital therapy.* New York: W. W. Norton.

Imber-Black E. (1989). Creating rituals in therapy (special issue). *The Family Therapy Networker, 13* (4).

Imber-Black, E. and Roberts, J. (1992). *Rituals for our times.* New York: HarperCollins.

Josselson, R. (1987). *Finding herself: Pathways to identity development in women.* San Francisco: Jossey-Bass.

Josselson, R. and Lieblich, A. (1993). *The narrative study of lives.* Newbury Park, Calif.: Sage.

Jung, C. G. (1963). *Modern man in search of a soul.* New York: Harcourt, Brace and World.

Kahana, B. and Kahana, E. (1983). New directions in assessement and treatment. In Lewinson, P. M. and Teri, L. (eds.) *Clinical Geropsychology.* New York: Pergamon Press.

Katcher, A. H. (1982). Are companion animals good for your health? A review of the evidence. *Aging,* 2–8.

Kaufman, S. R. (1986). *The ageless self: Sources of meaning in late life.* New York: Meridian.

Kaufman, S. R. and Becker, G. (1991). Content and boundaries of medicine in long-term care: Physicians talk about stroke. *The Gerontologist, 31,* 238–245.

Kazin, A. (1956). *Selected stories of Sholom Aleichem.* New York: Modern Library.

Kerr, M. E. and Bowen, M. (1988). *Family evaluation: An approach based on Bowen theory.* New York: W. W. Norton.

Kiesler, C. A. (1992). U.S. Mental health policy: Doomed to fail. *American Psychologist, 47,* 1077–1082.

Kleinman, A. (1988). *The illness narratives: Suffering, healing and the healing condition.* New York: Basic Books.

Knight, B. G. (1992). *Older adults in psychotherapy: Case histories.* London: Sage.

Knight, B. G. (1986). *Psychotherapy with older adults.* London: Sage.

Kobasa, S. C. (1979). Stressful life events, personality, and health: An inquiry into hardiness. *Journal of Personality and Social Psychology, 37,* 1–11.

Kobasa, S. C., Maddi, S. R. and Kahn, S. (1982). Hardiness and health: A prospective study. *Journal of Personality and Social Psychology, 42,* 168–177.

Koening, H. G. (1994). *Aging and God: Spiritual pathways to mental health in midlife and later years.* New York: Haworth.

Konner, M. (1993). *Medicine at the crossroads.* New York: Pantheon.

Konner, M. (1987). *Becoming a doctor: A journey of initiation in medical school.* New York: Viking.

Levinson, D. J. (1996). *The seasons of a woman's life.* New York: Alfred A. Knopf.

Levinson, D. J. (1986). A conception of adult development. *American Psychologist, 41,* 3–13.

Levinson, D. J. (1978). *The seasons of a man's life.* New York: Alfred A. Knopf.

Lewis, C. S. (1989). *A grief observed.* New York: HarperCollins.

Liddiard, R. N. and Ritvo, R. A. (1986). Self care in health policy: A conflict of interest. In Dean, K. (ed.), *Self care and health in old age* (pp. 298–319). London: Croom Elm.

Lidz, T. (1983). *The person: His and her development through the life cycle.* New York: Basic Books.

Linn, M., Fabricant, S. and Linn, F. (1988). *Healing the eight stages of life.* Mahwah, N.J.: Paulist Press.

London, P. (1986). *The modes and morals of psychotherapy.* New York: Harper and Row.

Lynch, J. J. (1979). *The broken heart: The medical consequences of loneliness.* New York: Harper and Row.

Mace, N. L. and Rabins, P. V. (1991). *The 36-hour day: A family guide to caring for a person with Alzheimer's.* Baltimore: Johns Hopkins University Press.

Maclay, E. (1977). *Green winter: Celebrations of old age.* New York: McGraw-Hill.

May, R. (1991). *The cry for myth.* New York: W. W. Norton.

May, R. (1975). *The courage to create.* New York: W. W. Norton.

Mays, D. T. and Franks, C. M. (1985). *Negative outcome in psychotherapy and what to do about it!* New York: Springer.

McDaniel, S. H., Gepworth, J. and Doherty, W. J. (1992). *Medical family therapy: A biopsychosocial approach to families with health problems.* New York: Basic Books.

McFadden, S. H. and Gerl, R. R. (1990). Approaches to understanding spirituality in the second half of life. *Generations, 14,* 35–38.

Michener, J. A. (1996). *This noble land: My vision for America.* Health care in a time of triage (Chapter 8). New York: Random House.

Millard, P. H. (1991). A case for the development of *gerocomy* in all district general hospitals. *Journal of the Royal Society of Medicine, 84,* 731–733.

Mills, E. S. (1993). *The story of Elderhostel.* Hanover, N.H.: University Press of New England.

Minuchin, S. and Nicholas, M. P. (1992). *Family healing.* New York: Free Press.

Moore, T. (1996). *The re-enchantment of everyday life.* New York: HarperCollins.

Moore, T. (1992). *Care of the soul.* New York: HarperCollins.

Murphy, M. J. (1996). *The Wizard of Oz* as cultural narrative and conceptual model for psychotherapy. *Psychotherapy, 33,* 531–538.

Muschel, I. J. (1984). Pet therapy with terminal cancer patients. *Social Casework, 65,* 8, 451–458.

Myers, M. F. (1994). *Doctor's marriages: A look at the problems and their solutions.* New York: Plenum.

Naughten, G. and Laidler, T. (1991). *When I grow too old to dream: Coping with Alzheimer's disease.* North Blackburn, Australia: Collins Dove (HarperCollins).

Nichols, M. P. (1995). *The lost art of listening.* New York: Guilford Press.

Niemeyer, R. A. and Mahoney, M. J. (1995). *Constructing realities: Meaning-making perspectives.* San Francisco: Jossey-Bass.

Nouwen, H. J. and Gaffney, W. J. (1974). *Aging: The fulfillment of life.* New York: Doubleday.

Nussbaum, D. (1996). On the verge of a major paradigm shift. *Clinical Geropsychology News* (APA Division 12), *3,* 5–9.

Omer, H. (1993). Short-term psychotherapy and the rise of the life sketch. *Psychotherapy, 30,* 668–673.

Orient, J. (1994). *Your doctor is not in.* New York: Crown.

Payne, B. P. (1990). Research and theoretical approaches to spirituality and aging. *Generations, 14,* 11–14.

Peake, T. H., Borduin, C. M. and Archer, R. P. (1988). *Brief psychotherapies: Changing frames of mind.* Beverly Hills, Calif.: Sage.

Peake, T. H. and Philpot, C. (1991). Psychotherapy with older adults: Hopes and fears. *The Clinical Supervisor, 9,* 185–202.

Peake, T. H., Rosenzweig, S. G. and Williamson, J. M. (1996). Aging problems and family solutions. In Harway, M. (ed.) *Understanding and treating the changing family.* New York: John Wiley.

Pittman, F. (1989). *Private lies: Infidelity and the betrayal of intimacy.* New York: W. W. Norton

Polster, E. (1987). *Every person's life is worth a novel.* New York: W. W. Norton.

Poon, L. W. (1986). *Aging in the 1980's: Psychological issues.* Washington, D.C.: American Psychological Association.

Poon, L. W. (ed.) (1986). *Clinical memory assessment of older adults.* Washington, D.C.: American Psychological Association.

Prest, L. A. and Keller, J. F. (1993). Spirituality and family therapy: Spiritual beliefs, myths and metaphors. *Journal of Marital and Family Therapy, 19,* 137–148.

Price, R. (1994). *A whole new life: An illness and a healing.* New York: Scribner.

Ptak, A. (1995). Access to healthcare facilities—Common sense must prevail. *Interactions* (Delta Society Newsletter), *13,* 2, 13–15.

Rebok, G. W. and Hoyer, W. J. (1977). The functional context of elderly behavior. *The Gerontologist, 17,* 27–34.

Retsinas, J. (1995). Back to the future—House calls. *Aging Today, 16,* 4, 1–2.

Robb, S., Boyd, M. and Pritash, C. L. (1980). A wine bottle, plant, and puppy: Catalysts for social behavior. *Journal of Gerontological Nursing, 6,* 721–728.

Roberto, L. G. (1992). *Transgenerational family therapies.* New York: Guilford Press.

Robinson, J.A.T. (1963.) *Honest to God.* Philadelphia: Westminister Press.

Rodin, J. and Langer, E. (1980). Aging labels: The decline of control and the fall of self-esteem. *Journal of Social Issues, 36,* 12–29.

Rosen, H. and Kuelwein, K. (eds.) (1996). *Constructing realities: Meaning—making perspectives for psychotherapists.* New York: Jossey-Bass.

Rybash, J. M., Hoyer, W. J. and Roodin, P. A. (1986). *Adult cognition and aging: Developmental changes in processing, knowing and thinking.* New York: Pergamon.

Sachs, K. (1993). Health care needs of the elderly: A comparison of the United States and United Kingdom using the Delphi Process. Graduate thesis. Florida Institute of Technology.

Scarf, M. (1987). *Intimate partners: Patterns in love and marriage.* New York: Ballantine.

Schaie, K. W. (1994). The course of adult intellectual development. *American Psychologist, 49,* 304–313.

Schover, L. R. (1986). Sexual problems. In Teri, L. and Lewinsohn, P. M. (eds.) *Geropsychological assessment and treatment.* New York: Springer.

Scully, T. and Scully, C. (1987). *Playing God: The new world of medical choices.* New York: Simon and Schuster.

Segal, D. (1964). The principle of minimal interference in the management of the elderly patient. *Journal of Chronic Disease, 17,* 299–300.

Sehulster, J. R. (1996). In my era: Evidence for the perception of a special period of the past. *Memory, 4,* 145–158. (Psychology Press, an imprint of Erlbaum (UK) Taylor and Francis Ltd.)

Seligman, M. (1995). The effectiveness of psychotherapy. *American Psychologist, 50,* 965–974.

Seligman, M. (1991). *Learned optimism.* New York: Alfred A. Knopf.

Seuss, Dr. (1986). *You're only old once!* New York: Random House.

Sheehy, G. (1995). *New passages: Mapping your life across time.* New York: Random House.

Sheehy, G. (1981). *Pathfinders.* New York: William Morrow.

Siegel, B. (1986). *Love, medicine and miracles.* New York: Harper and Row.

Siegel, J. M. (1990). Stressful life events and use of physician services among the elderly: The moderating role of pet ownership. *Journal of Personality and Social Psychology, 58,* 1081–1086.

Singer, I. B. (1970). *A crown of feathers and other stories.* New York: Farrar, Straus and Giroux

Skynner, R. and Cleese, J. (1984). *Families and how to survive them.* Oxford: Oxford University Press.

Stoddard, S. (1992). *The hospice movement: A better way of caring for the dying.* New York: Vintage.

Stokols, D. (1992). Establishing and maintaining healthy environments. *American Psychologist, 47,* 6–22.

Stone, R. (1994). *Stories: The family legacy.* Maitland, Fla.: Story Work Institute Press.

Storandt, M. and Vandenbos, G. R. (eds.) (1989). *The adult years: Continuity and change.* Washington, D.C.: American Psychological Association.

Strupp, H. H. (1996). The tripartite model and the *Consumer Reports* study. *American Psychologist, 51,* 1017–1024.

Strupp, H. H., Hadley, S. W. and Gomes-Schwartz, B. (1977). *Psychotherapy for better or worse: An analysis of the problem of negative effects.* New York: Jason Aronson.

Thomas, D. (1946). *Collected poems.* New York: New Directions.

Thomas, E. M. (1993). *The hidden life of dogs.* New York: Houghton Mifflin.

Thompson, E. H. (ed.) (1994). *Older men's lives.* Thousand Oaks, Calif.: Sage.

Turner, B. F. and Troll, L. E. (1994). *Women growing older.* Thousand Oaks, Calif.: Sage.

Vaillant, G. E. (1993). *The wisdom of the ego.* Cambridge, Mass.: Harvard University Press.

Vaillant, G. E. (1977). *Adaptation to life.* Boston: Little, Brown and Co.

Vash, C. L. (1994). *Personality and adversity: Psychospiritual aspects of rehabilitation.* New York: Springer.

Viney, L. L. (1993). *Life stories: Personal construct therapy with the elderly.* New York: John Wiley.

Viorst, J. (1986). *Necessary losses.* New York: Ballantine.

Waitzkin, H. (1991). *The politics of medical encounters.* New Haven, Conn.: Yale University Press.

Weisil, E. (1966). *The gates of the forest.* New York: Avon Books.

Wettle, T. (1989). Age as a risk factor for inadequate treatment. *Journal of the American Medical Association, 258,* 516.

Wilson, H. (1976). *The governance of Britain.* New York: Harper and Row.

Wulf, D. M. (1991). *Psychology of religion: Classic and contemporary views.* New York: John Wiley.

Yalom, I. (1980). *Existential psychotherapy.* New York: Basic Books.

Index

About the Author

THOMAS H. PEAKE is Professor of Psychology at Florida Tech and an adjunct professor at the Florida Mental Health Institute. Licensed in three states and England, he has trained health professionals and practiced clinical psychology for over 20 years. His publication and practice areas include books and articles in psychotherapy, clinical training, medical psychology, couples therapy and healthy aging.